THE

NINJA FOODI XL PRO

AIR FRYER OVEN

COOKBOOK

1000-DAY EASY AND AFFORDABLE AIR FRYER OVEN RECIPES TO BAKE, FRY, TOAST THE BEST MEALS

ERICK DAVIS

CONTENTS

INTRODUCTION

How Does the Ninja Foodi XL Pro Air Fryer Oven Work?

Air fryer is an oven feature that works like a countertop air fryer. Inside an air fryer oven, super-heated air circulates around the food to provide crispy, golden results without all the oil that deep-frying requires.

Air fryer ovens eliminate the need for another countertop appliance by putting the same technology right in your oven.

The Benefits of The Ninja Foodi XL Pro Air Fryer Oven

During the last few years, these appliances are arguably the most respected and trendy thing that is happening in the kitchen. In comparison to other ways of frying, there are several benefits to use an air fryer.

1. The Ninja Foodi XL Pro Air Fryer Oven May Stimulate Weight Loss

Higher intakes of fried foods are closely related to a higher risk of obesity. It is because deep-fried foods happen to be rich in fat and calories. Swapping from deep-fried foods to air-fried foods and reducing the daily consumption of unsanitary oils will help to minimize weight loss.

2. The Ninja Foodi XL Pro Air fryer Oven May Be More Stable Than Deep Fryers

Heating a huge container full of scalding oil requires deep-frying foods. This could pose a danger to defense. There is no chance of wasting, splashing, or inadvertently hitting hot oil as air fryers get hot. People should carefully use frying machines and follow guidelines to ensure safety.

3. The Ninja Foodi XL Pro Air fryer Oven May Save Lots of Space

You could enjoy this advantage if you have a tiny kitchen, or live in a dorm room or communal housing. These systems are often the size of a coffee maker. They do not take up too much space on the fridge, and it is typically easy to store or pass about.

4. The Quality of Electricity

These fryers are more powerful than an oven, and they are not going to heat up your home.

Using Tips for the Ninja Foodi XL Pro Air Fryer Oven

1. Use the Right Cookware

A perforated pan (sometimes called a perforated crisper tray) allows air to circulate under and around your food for even crisping. If you don't have one, you can use an oven-safe cooling rack. Line the bottom of your oven with aluminum foil or put a baking sheet under the rack below to catch any drips or crumbs.

2. Spread Out the Food

If you overload your pan to the point where food is piled up or touching, the exteriors won't brown as well, and it will steam instead of bake or air-fry. Instead, spread it in an even layer with plenty of room between each piece for air to circulate.

3. Cut Your Food Wisely

There's a reason why french fries are in long sticks — it's because this shape maximizes their surface, providing plenty of exterior for browning. Cut foods into long sticks or small, bite-sized pieces. If you are cooking something like tofu, try tearing it into pieces instead of slicing. The craggy shape will encourage the jagged edges to get crisp and brown.

4. Prepare Food Properly

The drier your food is before it goes into the oven, the better. Also, spraying it lightly with cooking spray or brushing or tossing with a neutral oil (like vegetable or grapeseed oil) will help encourage browning and crisping and will give a hint of that deep-fried taste we love.

5. Be Sure to Flip

Air fryer recipes usually recommend flipping the food halfway through cooking. This helps it cook and brown evenly. Don't omit this step in the instructions if you're using a convection or regular oven. After you flip, spritzing the other side with more cooking spray will also ensure both sides are equally crisp.

6. Know How to Adjust a Recipe

Air fryers cook hotter and faster than a conventional oven, so be aware that your recipe might take a few minutes longer. Start checking it for doneness at the time indicated in the recipe, and if it doesn't look browned enough, check every three minutes until it's golden brown and delicious!

In terms of temperature, air fryer recipes usually recommend a temperature of 20 to 25 degrees lower than you'd cook that type of food in a conventional oven, but the same holds true for convection ovens, so you can likely use the same temperature setting in an air fryer recipe for your convection oven. Cooking in a regular oven or toaster oven without a convection fan? Crank up the temperature by 25 degrees and make sure the oven is fully preheated before putting the food inside.

Tips on Cleaning Your Ninja Foodi XL Pro Air Fryer Oven

Along with the racks, your oven interior, exterior, and trays also require regular cleaning if the appliance is used frequently. Here are a few oven cleaning tips that you might find helpful:

- Remove and soak panel knobs in water and dish soap; this allows for thorough cleaning of both, the panel and knobs
- Use the self-cleaning option if your oven has one
- Stubborn grime on interior walls of your oven can be loosened and removed by spraying with a warm solution of 3 part water to 1 part vinegar; wipe with a damp cloth thereafter
- Fill the tray with hot soapy water and scrub when the water cools down
- Clean the inner glass door with a layer of water and baking soda paste (leave to sit for 15 minutes); wipe with a soft, damp cloth to remove traces of the baking soda
- Clean the exteriors glass with vinegar and water, or an eco-friendly glass cleaning product
- Be extremely careful with oven cleaner on natural stone surfaces, it makes it very easy to damage
- Even after utilizing commercial products with instructions, there's still a chance to damage your oven. Be careful spraying oven cleaner on stainless steel surfaces.

BREAKFAST

Apple Incredibles

Servings: 6

Cooking Time: 25 Minutes

Ingredients:

- Muffin mixture:
- 2 cups unbleached flour
- 1 teaspoon baking powder
- ¼ cup brown sugar
- ½ teaspoon salt
- ¼ cup margarine, at room temperature
- ½ cup skim milk
- 1 egg, beaten
- 2 tablespoons finely chopped raisins
- 2 tablespoons finely chopped pecans
- 1 apple, peeled, cored, and thinly sliced

Directions:

1. Preheat the toaster oven to 400° F.
2. Combine the muffin mixture ingredients in a large bowl, stirring just to blend. Fill the pans of an oiled or nonstick 6-muffin tin with the batter. Insert the apple slices vertically into the batter, standing and pushing them all the way down to the bottom of the pan.
3. BAKE for 25 minutes, or until the apples are tender and the muffins are lightly browned.

Breakfast Bars

Servings: 6

Cooking Time: 35 Minutes

Ingredients:

- 1 cup unsweetened applesauce
- 1 carrot, peeled and grated
- ½ cup raisins
- 1 egg
- 1 tablespoon vegetable oil
- 2 tablespoons molasses
- 2 tablespoons brown sugar
- ¼ cup chopped walnuts
- 2 cups rolled oats
- 2 tablespoons sesame seeds
- 1 teaspoon ground cinnamon
- ¼ teaspoon grated nutmeg
- ¼ teaspoon ground ginger
- Salt to taste

Directions:

1. Preheat the toaster oven to 375° F.
2. Combine all the ingredients in a bowl, stirring well to blend. Press the mixture into an oiled or nonstick 8½ × 8½ × 2inch square baking (cake) pan.
3. BAKE for 35 minutes, or until golden brown. Cool and cut into squares.

Sheet Pan French Toast

Servings: 2

Cooking Time: 15 Minutes

Ingredients:

- Oil spray (hand-pumped)
- 2 large eggs
- ¼ cup milk
- 1 teaspoon vanilla extract
- ¼ teaspoon ground cinnamon
- 4 slices whole-grain bread
- ¾ cup maple syrup, or to taste

Directions:

1. Preheat the toaster oven on BAKE to 350°F for 5 minutes.
2. Line the baking tray with parchment paper and generously spray the paper with oil.
3. In a medium bowl, whisk the eggs, milk, vanilla, and cinnamon until well blended.
4. Dredge a slice of bread in the egg mixture until submerged, turn, and take it out. Gently shake the bread to remove any excess egg mixture and place the bread on the baking sheet. Repeat with the remaining bread.
5. Bake for 10 minutes.
6. Flip the bread and bake for 5 minutes longer until both sides are golden brown and crispy.
7. Serve with maple syrup.

Bread Boat Eggs

Servings: 4

Cooking Time: 10 Minutes

Ingredients:

- 4 pistolette rolls
- 1 teaspoon butter
- ¼ cup diced fresh mushrooms
- ½ teaspoon dried onion flakes
- 4 eggs
- ½ teaspoon salt
- ¼ teaspoon dried dill weed
- ¼ teaspoon dried parsley
- 1 tablespoon milk

Directions:

1. Cut a rectangle in the top of each roll and scoop out center, leaving ½-inch shell on the sides and bottom.
2. Place butter, mushrooms, and dried onion in air fryer oven baking pan and air-fry for 1 minute. Stir and cook 3 more minutes.
3. In a medium bowl, beat together the eggs, salt, dill, parsley, and milk. Pour mixture into pan with mushrooms.
4. Air-fry at 390°F for 2 minutes. Stir. Continue cooking for 3 or 4 minutes, stirring every minute, until eggs are scrambled to your liking.
5. Remove baking pan from air fryer oven and fill rolls with scrambled egg mixture.
6. Place filled rolls in air fryer oven and air-fry at 390°F for 2 to 3 minutes or until rolls are lightly browned.

Berry Crisp

Servings: 4

Cooking Time: 25 Minutes

Ingredients:

- 2 16-ounce packages frozen berries or 4 cups fresh berries
- 2 tablespoons lemon juice
- ½ cup rolled oats
- 1 tablespoon margarine, at room temperature
- 3 tablespoons wheat germ
- 4 ¼ cup honey
- 5 1 teaspoon vanilla extract
- Salt to taste

Directions:

1. Preheat the toaster oven to 400° F.
2. Combine the berries or fruit and lemon juice in a 1-quart-size 8½ × 8½ × 4-inch ovenproof baking dish, tossing well to mix. Set aside.
3. Combine the rolled oats, margarine, wheat germ, honey, vanilla, and salt in a small bowl and stir with a fork until the mixture is crumbly. Sprinkle evenly on top of the berries.
4. BAKE, covered, for 20 minutes, or until the berries are bubbling. Remove from the oven and uncover.
5. BROIL for 5 minutes, or until the topping is lightly browned.

Italian Strata

Servings: 6

Cooking Time: 55 Minutes

Ingredients:

- 1 cup boiling water
- 3 tablespoons chopped sun-dried tomatoes (dry-packed)
- 5 cups cubed French bread or country bread (cut into 1-inch cubes)
- Nonstick cooking spray
- 1 ½ ounces sliced turkey pepperoni, cut into fourths (about ¾ cup)
- 2 tablespoons chopped pepperoncini peppers
- 1 cup coarsely chopped fresh spinach
- 1 cup shredded Italian blend cheese or mozzarella cheese
- 4 large eggs
- 1 ½ cups whole milk
- 1 teaspoon Italian seasoning
- ¼ teaspoon kosher salt
- 2 tablespoons shredded Parmesan cheese

Directions:

1. Pour the boiling water the over sun-dried tomatoes in a small, deep bowl; set aside.
2. Preheat the toaster oven to 350 °F. Place the bread cubes on a 12 x 12-inch baking pan. Bake for 10 minutes, stirring once.
3. Spray an 8 x 8-inch square baking pan with nonstick cooking spray. Drain the sun-dried tomatoes and pat dry with paper towels. Arrange half the bread cubes evenly in the prepared pan. Top with half the pepperoni, half the pepperoncini, all the spinach, and all of the reconstituted tomatoes. Sprinkle with ½ cup of the Italian cheese. Repeat layers with the remaining bread, pepperoni, pepperoncini, and ½ cup cheese.
4. Whisk the eggs, milk, Italian seasoning, and salt in a large bowl. Pour the egg mixture over the bread layers. Press down lightly with the back of a large spoon. Sprinkle with the Parmesan cheese. Cover and chill for at least 2 hours or overnight.
5. Preheat the toaster oven to 350°F. Bake the strata, uncovered, for 35 to 45 minutes, or until a knife inserted into the center comes out clean. Let stand for 10 minutes before serving.

Bacon Cheddar Biscuits

Servings: 6

Cooking Time: 15 Minutes

Ingredients:

- 1 cup all-purpose flour
- 1 tablespoon baking powder
- ¼ teaspoon table salt
- ¼ teaspoon smoked paprika or freshly ground black pepper
- 3 tablespoons unsalted butter
- ½ cup whole milk
- 1 cup shredded sharp cheddar cheese
- 2 tablespoons minced fresh chives
- 4 slices bacon, cooked until crisp and crumbled

Directions:

1. Preheat the toaster oven to 425°F.
2. Stir the flour, baking powder, salt, and paprika in a large bowl. Using a pastry cutter or two knives, cut the butter into the flour mixture until the mixture is crumbly throughout. Pour in the milk and gently mix until just combined. Stir in the cheese, chives, and bacon.
3. Turn the dough onto a lightly floured surface and knead lightly about 8 times. Roll the dough, using a rolling pin, until about ¾ inch thick. Cut out rounds using a 2-inch cutter. Place 1 inch apart on an ungreased 12 x 12-inch baking pan. Bake for 12 to 15 minutes or until golden brown.

Orange Rolls

Servings: 8

Cooking Time: 10 Minutes

Ingredients:

- parchment paper
- 3 ounces low-fat cream cheese
- 1 tablespoon low-fat sour cream or plain yogurt (not Greek yogurt)
- 2 teaspoons sugar
- ¼ teaspoon pure vanilla extract
- ¼ teaspoon orange extract
- 1 can (8 count) organic crescent roll dough
- ¼ cup chopped walnuts
- ¼ cup dried cranberries
- ¼ cup shredded, sweetened coconut
- butter-flavored cooking spray
- Orange Glaze
- ½ cup powdered sugar
- 1 tablespoon orange juice
- ¼ teaspoon orange extract
- dash of salt

Directions:

1. Cut a circular piece of parchment paper slightly smaller than the bottom of your air fryer oven. Set aside.
2. In a small bowl, combine the cream cheese, sour cream or yogurt, sugar, and vanilla and orange extracts. Stir until smooth.
3. Preheat the toaster oven to 300°F.
4. Separate crescent roll dough into 8 triangles and divide cream cheese mixture among them. Starting at wide end, spread cheese mixture to within 1 inch of point.
5. Sprinkle nuts and cranberries evenly over cheese mixture.
6. Starting at wide end, roll up triangles, then sprinkle with coconut, pressing in lightly to make it stick. Spray tops of rolls with butter-flavored cooking spray.
7. Place parchment paper in air fryer oven, and place 4 rolls on top, spaced evenly.
8. Air-fry for 10minutes, until rolls are golden brown and cooked through.
9. Repeat steps 7 and 8 to cook remaining 4 rolls. You should be able to use the same piece of parchment paper twice.
10. In a small bowl, stir together ingredients for glaze and drizzle over warm rolls.

Breakfast Pizza

Servings: 2

Cooking Time: 60 Minutes

Ingredients:

- 3 tablespoons extra-virgin olive oil, divided, plus extra for drizzling
- 1 recipe Classic Pizza Dough (recipe follows), room temperature
- 4 ounces whole-milk mozzarella cheese, shredded (1 cup)
- ½ ounce Parmesan cheese, grated (¼ cup)
- 2 ounces (¼ cup) cottage cheese
- ⅛ teaspoon dried oregano
- 4 ounces breakfast sausage, casings removed
- 4 large eggs
- ⅛ teaspoon table salt
- ⅛ teaspoon pepper
- 2 tablespoons minced fresh chive

Directions:

1. Coat small rimmed baking sheet with 2 tablespoons oil. Press and roll dough into 11 by 8-inch rectangle on lightly floured counter. (If dough springs back during rolling, let rest for 10 minutes before rolling again.) Transfer dough to prepared sheet and re-stretch dough into 11 by 8-inch rectangle. Brush dough evenly with 1 teaspoon oil and cover with plastic wrap. Let sit in warm spot until slightly risen, about 20 minutes.
2. Adjust toaster oven rack to lowest position and preheat the toaster oven to 450 degrees. Remove plastic and, using your fingers, make indentations all over dough. Bake until dough has puffed slightly, 5 to 7 minutes.
3. Combine mozzarella and Parmesan in bowl. Combine cottage cheese, oregano, and remaining 2 teaspoons oil in separate bowl.
4. Remove sheet from oven and, using spatula, press down on any air bubbles. Spread cottage cheese mixture evenly over top, leaving ½-inch border around edges. Pinch sausage into dime-size pieces and arrange evenly over cottage cheese mixture. Sprinkle mozzarella mixture evenly over pizza, leaving ½-inch border. Using back of spoon, create 4 evenly spaced indentations in cheese, each about 3 inches in diameter. Crack 1 egg into each well, then sprinkle with salt and pepper.
5. Bake until crust is golden brown on bottom and eggs are just set, 9 to 10 minutes for slightly runny yolks or 11 to 12 minutes for soft but set yolks. Remove pizza from pan and transfer to wire rack; let rest for 5 minutes. Sprinkle with chives and drizzle with extra oil. Cut into 8 equal pieces and serve.

Cherry Almond Scones

Servings: 12

Cooking Time: 25 Minutes

Ingredients:

- 2 3/4 cups all-purpose flour
- 1/2 cup sugar
- 1 tablespoon baking powder
- 3/4 teaspoon salt
- 1 cup dried cherries
- 1 cup slivered almonds
- 1/2 cup cold butter, sliced into tablespoons
- 2 large eggs
- 1/2 cup sour cream
- 1 teaspoon almond extract
- 1/2 teaspoon vanilla extract
- 1 tablespoon milk
- Coarse sugar

Directions:

1. Preheat the toaster oven to 375°F.
2. In a large mixer bowl, stir flour, sugar, baking powder and salt until blended.
3. Add butter pieces. Beat on MEDIUM speed until mixture is crumbly with some larger pieces of butter.
4. In a large mixer bowl on MEDIUM-HIGH speed, beat eggs, sour cream, almond extract and vanilla extract until blended.
5. Stir into flour mixture until mixture is blended and no longer dry. Lightly knead in cherries and almonds.
6. Divide dough in half. Form each into circles about 3/4-inch thick on parchment-lined baking sheet.
7. Brush each circle with milk and sprinkle tops with coarse sugar. Using a floured metal spatula, cut each circle into 6 wedges. Separate the wedges, leaving 1/2-inch between each wedge.
8. Bake for 20 to 25 minutes or until golden brown. Cool for 15 minutes before serving.

FISH AND SEAFOOD

Baked Tomato Pesto Bluefish

Servings: 2

Cooking Time: 23 Minutes

Ingredients:

- 2 plum tomatoes
- 2 tablespoons tomato paste
- ¼ cup fresh basil leaves
- 1 tablespoon olive oil
- 2 garlic cloves
- 2 tablespoons pine nuts
- ¼ cup grated Parmesan cheese
- 1 teaspoon dried oregano
- Salt to taste
- 2 6-ounce bluefish fillets

Directions:

1. Preheat the toaster oven to 400° F.
2. Process the pesto ingredients in a blender or food processor until smooth.
3. Place the bluefish fillets in an oiled or nonstick 8½ × 8½ × 2-inch square baking (cake) pan.
4. BAKE, covered, for 15 minutes, or until the fish flakes with a fork. Remove from the oven, uncover, and spread the pesto mixture on both sides of the fillets.
5. BROIL, uncovered, for 8 minutes, or until the pesto is lightly browned.

Broiled Lemon Coconut Shrimp

Servings: 4

Cooking Time: 10 Minutes

Ingredients:

- Brushing mixture:
- 2 tablespoons lemon juice
- 4 tablespoons olive oil
- 1 tablespoon grated lemon zest
- Salt to taste
- 1 pound fresh shrimp, peeled, deveined, and butterflied
- ½ cup grated unsweetened coconut

Directions:

1. Combine the brushing mixture ingredients in a small bowl. Add the shrimp and toss to coat well. Set aside.
2. Place the coconut on a plate, spreading it out evenly.
3. Press each shrimp into the coconut, coating well on all sides. Place the shrimp in an 8½ × 8½ × 2-inch oiled or nonstick square (cake) pan.
4. BROIL the shrimp for 5 minutes, turn with tongs, and broil for 5 more minutes, or until browned lightly.

Coconut-shrimp Po' Boys

Servings: 4

Cooking Time: 5 Minutes

Ingredients:

- ½ cup cornstarch
- 2 eggs
- 2 tablespoons milk
- ¾ cup shredded coconut
- ½ cup panko breadcrumbs
- 1 pound (31–35 count) shrimp, peeled and deveined
- Old Bay Seasoning
- oil for misting or cooking spray
- 2 large hoagie rolls
- honey mustard or light mayonnaise
- 1½ cups shredded lettuce
- 1 large tomato, thinly sliced

Directions:

1. Place cornstarch in a shallow dish or plate.
2. In another shallow dish, beat together eggs and milk.
3. In a third dish mix the coconut and panko crumbs.
4. Sprinkle shrimp with Old Bay Seasoning to taste.
5. Dip shrimp in cornstarch to coat lightly, dip in egg mixture, shake off excess, and roll in coconut mixture to coat well.
6. Spray both sides of coated shrimp with oil or cooking spray.
7. Cook half the shrimp in a single layer at 390°F for 5 minutes.
8. Repeat to cook remaining shrimp.
9. To Assemble
10. Split each hoagie lengthwise, leaving one long edge intact.
11. Place in air fryer oven and air-fry at 390°F for 1 to 2 minutes or until heated through.
12. Remove buns, break apart, and place on 4 plates, cut side up.
13. Spread with honey mustard and/or mayonnaise.
14. Top with shredded lettuce, tomato slices, and coconut shrimp.

Roasted Fish With Provençal Crumb Topping

Servings: 3

Cooking Time: 25 Minutes

Ingredients:

- 1 tablespoon olive oil, plus more for greasing
- ⅓ cup finely chopped onion
- 1 clove garlic, minced
- ¾ cup fresh bread crumbs
- 2 tablespoons chopped fresh flat-leaf (Italian) parsley
- 1 teaspoon fresh thyme leaves
- 3 (5-ounce) cod fillets, or other white-fleshed, mild-flavored fish, patted dry (about 1 ¼ inches thick)
- 2 tablespoons dry white wine
- 2 teaspoons fresh lemon juice

Directions:

1. Preheat the toaster oven to 400°F. Lightly grease the baking pan with olive oil.
2. Heat the tablespoon of olive oil in a small skillet over medium-high heat. Add the onion and cook, stirring frequently, for 3 to 4 minutes, or until tender. Add the garlic and cook for 30 seconds. Remove the skillet from the heat. Stir in the bread crumbs, parsley, and thyme.
3. Place the fish in the prepared pan. Drizzle with the wine. Divide the crumb mixture evenly over the top of each fish fillet, and press onto the fillets. Roast for 20 to 25 minutes, or until the top is brown and the fish is opaque and flakes easily when tested with a fork. Sprinkle the lemon juice evenly over the fish.

Lightened-up Breaded Fish Filets

Servings: 4

Cooking Time: 10 Minutes

Ingredients:

- ½ cup all-purpose flour
- ½ teaspoon cayenne pepper
- 1 teaspoon garlic powder
- ½ teaspoon black pepper
- ¼ teaspoon salt
- 2 eggs, whisked
- 1½ cups panko breadcrumbs
- 1 pound boneless white fish filets
- 1 cup tartar sauce
- 1 lemon, sliced into wedges

Directions:

1. In a medium bowl, mix the flour, cayenne pepper, garlic powder, pepper, and salt.
2. In a shallow dish, place the eggs.
3. In a third dish, place the breadcrumbs.
4. Cover the fish in the flour, dip them in the egg, and coat them with panko. Repeat until all fish are covered in the breading.
5. Liberally spray the metal trivet that fits inside the air fryer oven with olive oil mist. Place the fish onto the trivet, leaving space between the filets to flip. Air-fry for 5 minutes, flip the fish, and cook another 5 minutes. Repeat until all the fish is cooked.
6. Serve warm with tartar sauce and lemon wedges.

Spicy Fish Street Tacos With Sriracha Slaw

Servings: 2

Cooking Time: 5 Minutes

Ingredients:

- Sriracha Slaw:
- ½ cup mayonnaise
- 2 tablespoons rice vinegar
- 1 teaspoon sugar
- 2 tablespoons sriracha chili sauce
- 5 cups shredded green cabbage
- ¼ cup shredded carrots
- 2 scallions, chopped
- salt and freshly ground black pepper
- Tacos:
- ½ cup flour
- 1 teaspoon chili powder
- ½ teaspoon ground cumin
- 1 teaspoon salt
- freshly ground black pepper
- ½ teaspoon baking powder
- 1 egg, beaten
- ¼ cup milk
- 1 cup breadcrumbs
- 1 pound mahi-mahi or snapper fillets
- 1 tablespoon canola or vegetable oil
- 6 (6-inch) flour tortillas
- 1 lime, cut into wedges

Directions:

1. Start by making the sriracha slaw. Combine the mayonnaise, rice vinegar, sugar, and sriracha sauce in a large bowl. Mix well and add the green cabbage, carrots, and scallions. Toss until all the vegetables are coated with the dressing and season with salt and pepper. Refrigerate the slaw until you are ready to serve the tacos.
2. Combine the flour, chili powder, cumin, salt, pepper and baking powder in a bowl. Add the egg and milk and mix until the batter is smooth. Place the breadcrumbs in shallow dish.
3. Cut the fish fillets into 1-inch wide sticks, approximately 4-inches long. You should have about 12 fish sticks total. Dip the fish sticks into the batter, coating all sides. Let the excess batter drip off the fish and then roll them in the breadcrumbs, patting the crumbs onto all sides of the fish sticks. Set the coated fish on a plate or baking sheet until all the fish has been coated.
4. Preheat the toaster oven to 400°F.
5. Spray the coated fish sticks with oil on all sides. Spray or brush the inside of the air fryer oven with oil and transfer the fish to the air fryer oven. Place as many sticks as you can in one layer, leaving a little room around each stick. Place any remaining sticks on top, perpendicular to the first layer.
6. Air-fry the fish for 3 minutes. Turn the fish sticks over and air-fry for an additional 2 minutes.

7. While the fish is air-frying, warm the tortilla shells either in a 350°F oven wrapped in foil or in a skillet with a little oil over medium-high heat for a couple minutes. Fold the tortillas in half and keep them warm until the remaining tortillas and fish are ready.
8. To assemble the tacos, place two pieces of the fish in each tortilla shell and top with the sriracha slaw. Squeeze the lime wedge over top and dig in.

Crispy Sweet-and-sour Cod Fillets

Servings: 3
Cooking Time: 12 Minutes

Ingredients:

- 1½ cups Plain panko bread crumbs (gluten-free, if a concern)
- 2 tablespoons Regular or low-fat mayonnaise (not fat-free; gluten-free, if a concern)
- ¼ cup Sweet pickle relish
- 3 4- to 5-ounce skinless cod fillets

Directions:

1. Preheat the toaster oven to 400°F.
2. Pour the bread crumbs into a shallow soup plate or a small pie plate. Mix the mayonnaise and relish in a small bowl until well combined. Smear this mixture all over the cod fillets. Set them in the crumbs and turn until evenly coated on all sides, even on the ends.
3. Set the coated cod fillets in the air fryer oven with as much air space between them as possible. They should not touch. Air-fry undisturbed for 12 minutes, or until browned and crisp.
4. Use a nonstick-safe spatula to transfer the cod pieces to a wire rack. Cool for only a minute or two before serving hot.

Crunchy Clam Strips

Servings: 3

Cooking Time: 8 Minutes

Ingredients:

- ½ pound Clam strips, drained
- 1 Large egg, well beaten
- ½ cup All-purpose flour
- ½ cup Yellow cornmeal
- 1½ teaspoons Table salt
- 1½ teaspoons Ground black pepper
- Up to ¾ teaspoon Cayenne
- Vegetable oil spray

Directions:

1. Preheat the toaster oven to 400°F.
2. Toss the clam strips and beaten egg in a bowl until the clams are well coated.
3. Mix the flour, cornmeal, salt, pepper, and cayenne in a large zip-closed plastic bag until well combined. Using a flatware fork or small kitchen tongs, lift the clam strips one by one out of the egg, letting any excess egg slip back into the rest. Put the strips in the bag with the flour mixture. Once all the strips are in the bag, seal it until the strips are well coated.
4. Use kitchen tongs to pick out the clam strips and lay them on a cutting board (leaving any extra flour mixture in the bag to be discarded). Coat the strips on both sides with vegetable oil spray.
5. When the machine is at temperature, spread the clam strips in the air fryer oven in one layer. They may touch in places, but try to leave as much air space as possible around them. Air-fry undisturbed for 8 minutes, or until brown and crunchy.
6. Gently dump the contents of the air fryer oven onto a serving platter. Cool for just a minute or two before serving hot.

Maple Balsamic Glazed Salmon

Servings: 4

Cooking Time: 10 Minutes

Ingredients:

- 4 (6-ounce) fillets of salmon
- salt and freshly ground black pepper
- vegetable oil
- ¼ cup pure maple syrup
- 3 tablespoons balsamic vinegar
- 1 teaspoon Dijon mustard

Directions:

1. Preheat the toaster oven to 400°F.
2. Season the salmon well with salt and freshly ground black pepper. Spray or brush the bottom of the air fryer oven with vegetable oil and place the salmon fillets inside. Air-fry the salmon for 5 minutes.
3. While the salmon is air-frying, combine the maple syrup, balsamic vinegar and Dijon mustard in a small saucepan over medium heat and stir to blend well. Let the mixture simmer while the fish is cooking. It should start to thicken slightly, but keep your eye on it so it doesn't burn.
4. Brush the glaze on the salmon fillets and air-fry for an additional 5 minutes. The salmon should feel firm to the touch when finished and the glaze should be nicely browned on top. Brush a little more glaze on top before removing and serving with rice and vegetables, or a nice green salad.

Broiled Dill And Lemon Salmon

Servings: 25

Cooking Time: 2 Minutes

Ingredients:

- Brushing mixture:
- 2 tablespoons lemon juice
- 2 tablespoons olive oil
- 1 tablespoon soy sauce
- 1 teaspoon dried dill or dill weed
- ½ teaspoon garlic powder
- 1 teaspoon soy sauce
- 2 6-ounce salmon steaks

Directions:

1. Combine the brushing mixture ingredients in a small bowl and brush the salmon steak tops, skin side down, liberally, reserving the remaining mixture. Let the steaks sit at room temperature for 10 minutes, then place on a broiling rack with a pan underneath.
2. BROIL 15 minutes, remove from the oven, and brush the steaks with the remaining mixture. Broil again for 5 minutes, or until the meat flakes easily with a fork.

Crab-stuffed Peppers

Servings: 4

Cooking Time: 45 Minutes

Ingredients:

- Filling:
- 1½ cups fresh crabmeat, chopped, or 2 6-ounce cans lump crabmeat, drained
- 4 plum tomatoes, chopped
- 2 4-ounce cans sliced mushrooms, drained well
- 4 tablespoons pitted and sliced black olives
- 2 tablespoons olive oil
- 2 garlic cloves, minced
- ½ teaspoon ground cumin
- Salt and freshly ground black pepper to taste
- 4 large bell peppers, tops cut off, seeds and membrane removed
- ½ cup shredded low-fat mozzarella cheese

Directions:

1. Preheat the toaster oven to 375° F.
2. Combine the filling ingredients in a bowl and adjust the seasonings. Spoon the mixture to generously fill each pepper. Place the peppers upright in an 8½ × 8½ × 2-inch oiled or nonstick square (cake) pan.
3. BAKE for 40 minutes, or until the peppers are tender. Remove from the oven and sprinkle the cheese in equal portions on top of the peppers.
4. BROIL 5 minutes, or until the cheese is melted.

Butternut Squash–wrapped Halibut Fillets

Servings: 3

Cooking Time: 11 Minutes

Ingredients:

- 15 Long spiralized peeled and seeded butternut squash strands
- 3 5- to 6-ounce skinless halibut fillets
- 3 tablespoons Butter, melted
- ¾ teaspoon Mild paprika
- ¾ teaspoon Table salt
- ¾ teaspoon Ground black pepper

Directions:

1. Preheat the toaster oven to 375°F .
2. Hold 5 long butternut squash strands together and wrap them around a fillet. Set it aside and wrap any remaining fillet(s).
3. Mix the melted butter, paprika, salt, and pepper in a small bowl. Brush this mixture over the squash-wrapped fillets on all sides.
4. When the machine is at temperature, set the fillets in the air fryer oven with as much air space between them as possible. Air-fry undisturbed for 10 minutes, or until the squash strands have browned but not burned. If the machine is at 360°F, you may need to add 1 minute to the cooking time. In any event, watch the fish carefully after the 8-minute mark.
5. Use a nonstick-safe spatula to gently transfer the fillets to a serving platter or plates. Cool for only a minute or so before serving.

SNACKS APPETIZERS AND SIDES

Cranberry Pecan Rice Pilaf

Servings: 8

Cooking Time: 75 Minutes

Ingredients:

- Nonstick cooking spray
- 2 tablespoons unsalted butter
- 1 shallot, chopped
- ⅔ cup long-grain brown rice, rinsed and drained
- ¼ cup chopped pecans
- 1 (14.5-ounce) can reduced-sodium chicken broth
- ½ cup dried sweetened cranberries
- 2 tablespoons minced fresh flat-leaf (Italian) parsley
- 1 tablespoon minced fresh rosemary leaves or 1 teaspoon dried rosemary leaves, crumbled
- Kosher salt and freshly ground black pepper

Directions:

1. Preheat the toaster oven to 375°F. Spray a 2-quart casserole with nonstick cooking spray.
2. Melt the butter in a large skillet over medium-high heat. Add the shallot and cook, stirring frequently, for 3 minutes. Stir in the rice and cook, stirring frequently, until the rice is beginning to toast. Stir in the pecans and cook until the rice is golden brown and the pecans are toasted. Stir in the broth and ⅓ cup water. Heat until it just begins to boil. Remove from the heat and stir in the cranberries, parsley, and rosemary. Season with salt and pepper. Spoon the rice mixture into the prepared casserole dish.
3. Cover and bake for 70 to 75 minutes or until the rice is tender.

Mozzarella-stuffed Arancini

Servings: 14

Cooking Time: 20 Minutes

Ingredients:

- Pie Crust
- 3½ cups low sodium chicken stock
- 4 tablespoons unsalted butter, divided
- 1 medium onion, finely chopped
- 2 garlic cloves, minced
- 1 cup arborio rice
- 1½ teaspoons kosher salt, plus more to taste
- ½ cup dry white wine
- 2 ounces finely grated Parmesan
- ¼ cup heavy cream
- 1 teaspoon freshly ground black pepper, plus more to taste
- 3 ounces low-moisture mozzarella, cut into ⅓-inch pieces
- 1½ cups panko breadcrumbs
- 2 tablespoons melted salted butter
- ½ cup all-purpose flour 2 large eggs, beaten Cooking spray
- Marinara sauce, for serving

Directions:

1. Simmer chicken stock in a pot, then keep warm on low heat.
2. Heat 2 tablespoons of unsalted butter in a medium saucepan over medium heat.
3. Add onions to the saucepan and cook for 5 minutes or until softened.
4. Add garlic and cook for 1 minute or until softened.
5. Add rice and 1½ teaspoons of kosher salt to the saucepan.
6. Cook the rice for 3 minutes or until the edges turn translucent.
7. Pour in the wine, stir, and cook for 3 minutes or until the wine is all evaporated and the rice looks dry.
8. Ladle in 1 cup of the warm chicken stock and bring to a simmer. Stirring often, cook the rice for 5 minutes or until liquid is absorbed. Repeat this process with another cup of chicken stock.
9. Add the remaining 1½ cups of chicken stock and cook, stirring often, for 10 minutes or until the rice is cooked through but toothsome and the liquid is mostly absorbed.
10. Remove the risotto from the heat and mix in Parmesan, heavy cream, black pepper, and the remaining two tablespoons of unsalted butter.
11. Season the risotto to taste with salt and black pepper.
12. Spread risotto in an even layer on a parchment-lined baking sheet and cover with plastic wrap.
13. Place the risotto in the fridge and chill for 4 hours.

14. Seperate the chilled risotto into 14 even pieces and form them into round patties about 2½ inches in diameter.
15. Place a piece of mozzarella in the center of a patty, pinch and shape the risotto so it completely encases the cheese, then roll into a ball. Repeat with each risotto patty.
16. Place the balls onto the baking sheet lined with fresh parchment paper, cover with plastic wrap, and place in the freezer for 15 minutes.
17. Place the panko breadcrumbs into a food processor and pulse until finely ground, then place into a bowl.
18. Mix the panko breadcrumbs with the melted salted butter until well combined.
19. Remove the risotto balls from the freezer and dredge in flour, dip in beaten eggs, then cover with breadcrumbs. Repeat this process with the rest of the balls. Set aside.
20. Preheat the toaster oven to 400°F.
21. Place the balls into the fry basket, spray them liberally with cooking spray, then insert the basket at mid position in the preheated oven.
22. Select the Air Fry function, adjust time to 20 minutes, and press Start/Pause.
23. Remove the arancini from the oven and serve with marinara sauce.

Avocado Fries

Servings: 8

Cooking Time: 8 Minutes

Ingredients:

- 2 medium avocados, firm but ripe
- 1 large egg
- ½ teaspoon garlic powder
- ¼ teaspoon cayenne pepper
- ¼ teaspoon salt
- ¾ cup almond flour
- ½ cup finely grated Parmesan cheese
- ½ cup gluten-free breadcrumbs

Directions:

1. Preheat the toaster oven to 370°F.
2. Rinse the outside of the avocado with water. Slice the avocado in half, slice it in half again, and then slice it in half once more to get 8 slices. Remove the outer skin. Repeat for the other avocado. Set the avocado slices aside.
3. In a small bowl, whisk the egg, garlic powder, cayenne pepper, and salt in a small bowl. Set aside.
4. In a separate bowl, pour the almond flour.
5. In a third bowl, mix the Parmesan cheese and breadcrumbs.
6. Carefully roll the avocado slices in the almond flour, then dip them in the egg wash, and coat them in the cheese and breadcrumb topping. Repeat until all 16 fries are coated.
7. Liberally spray the air fryer oven with olive oil spray and place the avocado fries into the air fryer oven, leaving a little space around the sides between fries. Depending on the size of your air fryer oven, you may need to cook these in batches.
8. Cook fries for 8 minutes, or until the outer coating turns light brown.
9. Carefully remove, repeat with remaining slices, and then serve warm.

Avocado Egg Rolls

Servings: 8

Cooking Time: 8 Minutes

Ingredients:

- 8 full-size egg roll wrappers
- 1 medium avocado, sliced into 8 pieces
- 1 cup cooked black beans, divided
- ½ cup mild salsa, divided
- ½ cup shredded Mexican cheese, divided
- ⅓ cup filtered water, divided
- ½ cup sour cream
- 1 teaspoon chipotle hot sauce

Directions:

1. Preheat the toaster oven to 400°F.
2. Place the egg roll wrapper on a flat surface and place 1 strip of avocado down in the center.
3. Top the avocado with 2 tablespoons of black beans, 1 tablespoon of salsa, and 1 tablespoon of shredded cheese.
4. Place two of your fingers into the water, and then moisten the four outside edges of the egg roll wrapper with water (so the outer edges will secure shut).
5. Fold the bottom corner up, covering the filling. Then secure the sides over the top, remembering to lightly moisten them so they stick. Tightly roll the egg roll up and moisten the final flap of the wrapper and firmly press it into the egg roll to secure it shut.
6. Repeat Steps 2–5 until all 8 egg rolls are complete.
7. When ready to cook, spray the air fryer oven with olive oil spray and place the egg rolls into the air fryer oven. Depending on the size and type of air fryer oven you have, you may need to do this in two sets.
8. Air-fry for 4 minutes, flip, and then cook the remaining 4 minutes.
9. Repeat until all the egg rolls are cooked. Meanwhile, mix the sour cream with the hot sauce to serve as a dipping sauce.
10. Serve warm.

Polenta Fries With Chili-lime Mayo

Servings: 4

Cooking Time: 28 Minutes

Ingredients:

- 2 teaspoons vegetable or olive oil
- ¼ teaspoon paprika
- 1 pound prepared polenta, cut into 3-inch x ½-inch sticks
- salt and freshly ground black pepper
- Chili-Lime Mayo
- ½ cup mayonnaise
- 1 teaspoon chili powder
- ¼ teaspoon ground cumin
- juice of half a lime
- 1 teaspoon chopped fresh cilantro
- salt and freshly ground black pepper

Directions:

1. Preheat the toaster oven to 400°F.
2. Combine the oil and paprika and then carefully toss the polenta sticks in the mixture.
3. Air-fry the polenta fries at 400°F for 15 minutes. Rotate the fries and continue to air-fry for another 13 minutes or until the fries have browned nicely. Season to taste with salt and freshly ground black pepper.
4. To make the chili-lime mayo, combine all the ingredients in a small bowl and stir well.
5. Serve the polenta fries warm with chili-lime mayo on the side for dipping.

Baked Coconut Shrimp With Curried Chutney

Servings: 8-10

Cooking Time: 11 Minutes

Ingredients:

- 1 cup chutney
- 2 Tablespoons sliced green onion
- 1/2 teaspoon ground curry
- 1/2 teaspoon crushed red pepper
- 2 Tablespoons all-purpose flour
- 1 teaspoon salt
- 1 cup panko breadcrumbs
- 3/4 cup sweetened shredded coconut
- 1 egg white
- 1 pound (16 to 20 count) extra jumbo shrimp
- Cilantro

Directions:

1. In a small bowl, stir chutney, green onion, curry and crushed red pepper until blended. Set aside.
2. Preheat the toaster oven to 450°F. Spray a baking pan with nonstick cooking spray. Set aside.
3. In a large resealable plastic bag, combine flour and salt.
4. Add panko breadcrumbs and coconut to bag. Seal and shake to combine.
5. In a medium bowl, whisk egg white until foamy.
6. Dip one shrimp at a time into egg white.
7. Place shrimp in crumb mixture and press mixture onto shrimp until well coated. Arrange in single layer in prepared baking pan.
8. Bake for 9 to 11 minutes or until crumbs are golden brown. Serve with chutney mixture. Garnish with cilantro.

Brazilian Cheese Bread (pão De Queijo)

Servings: 8

Cooking Time: 18 Minutes

Ingredients:

- 1 large egg, room temperature
- ⅓ cup olive oil
- ⅔ cups whole milk 1½ cups tapioca flour
- ½ cup feta cheese
- ¼ cup Parmesan cheese
- 1 teaspoon kosher salt
- ¼ teaspoon garlic powder
- Cooking spray

Directions:

1. Blend the egg, olive oil, milk, tapioca flour, feta, Parmesan, salt, and garlic powder in a stand mixer until smooth.
2. Spray the mini muffin pan with cooking spray.
3. Pour the batter into the muffin cups so they are ¾ full.
4. .Preheat the toaster oven to 380°F.
5. Place the muffin pan on the wire rack, then insert rack at mid position in the preheated oven.
6. Select the Bake function, adjust time to 18 minutes, and press Start/Pause.
7. Remove when done, then carefully pop the bread from the mini muffin tin and serve.

Maple-glazed Acorn Squash

Servings: 2

Cooking Time: 30 Minutes

Ingredients:

- 1 acorn squash (1½ pounds), halved pole to pole, seeded, and cut into 8 wedges
- 1 tablespoon vegetable oil
- 1 teaspoon sugar
- ¼ teaspoon plus pinch table salt, divided
- ¼ teaspoon pepper
- 2 tablespoons maple syrup
- 2 tablespoons unsalted butter
- Pinch cayenne pepper
- 1 teaspoon fresh thyme leaves (optional)

Directions:

1. Adjust toaster oven rack to middle position and preheat the toaster oven to 450 degrees. Toss squash, oil, sugar, ¼ teaspoon salt, and pepper together on small rimmed baking sheet, then arrange cut side down in single layer. Roast until bottoms of squash wedges are deep golden brown, 15 to 20 minutes.
2. Meanwhile, microwave maple syrup, butter, cayenne, and remaining pinch salt in bowl, stirring occasionally, until butter is melted and mixture is slightly thickened, about 90 seconds; cover to keep warm.
3. Remove sheet from oven, and, using spatula, carefully flip squash. Brush with half of glaze and continue to roast until squash is tender and deep golden, 5 to 8 minutes. Carefully flip squash and brush with remaining glaze. Transfer squash to serving platter and sprinkle with thyme, if using. Serve.

Buffalo Bites

Servings: 16

Cooking Time: 12 Minutes

Ingredients:

- 1 pound ground chicken
- 8 tablespoons buffalo wing sauce
- 2 ounces Gruyère cheese, cut into 16 cubes
- 1 tablespoon maple syrup

Directions:

1. Mix 4 tablespoons buffalo wing sauce into all the ground chicken.
2. Shape chicken into a log and divide into 16 equal portions.
3. With slightly damp hands, mold each chicken portion around a cube of cheese and shape into a firm ball. When you have shaped 8 meatballs, place them in air fryer oven.
4. Air-fry at 390°F for approximately 5 minutes. Reduce temperature to 360°F, and air-fry for 5 minutes longer.
5. While the first batch is cooking, shape remaining chicken and cheese into 8 more meatballs.
6. Repeat step 4 to cook second batch of meatballs.
7. In a medium bowl, mix the remaining 4 tablespoons of buffalo wing sauce with the maple syrup. Add all the cooked meatballs and toss to coat.
8. Place meatballs back into air fryer oven and air-fry at 390°F for 2 minutes to set the glaze. Skewer each with a toothpick and serve.

Crab Rangoon

Servings: 18

Cooking Time: 6 Minutes

Ingredients:

- 4½ tablespoons (a little more than ¼ pound) Crabmeat, preferably backfin or claw, picked over for shells and cartilage
- 1½ ounces (3 tablespoons) Regular or low-fat cream cheese (not fat-free), softened to room temperature
- 1½ tablespoons Minced scallion
- 1½ teaspoons Minced garlic
- 1½ teaspoons Worcestershire sauce
- 18 Wonton wrappers (thawed, if necessary)
- Vegetable oil spray

Directions:

1. Preheat the toaster oven to 400°F.
2. Gently stir the crab, cream cheese, scallion, garlic, and Worcestershire sauce in a medium bowl until well combined.
3. Set a bowl of water on a clean, dry work surface or next to a large cutting board. Set one wonton wrapper on the surface, then put a teaspoonful of the crab mixture in the center of the wrapper. Dip your clean finger in the water and run it around the edge of the wrapper. Bring all four sides up to the center and over the filling, and pinch them together in the middle to seal without covering all of the filling. The traditional look is for the corners of the filled wonton to become four open "flower petals" radiating out from the filled center. Set the filled wonton aside and continue making more as needed. (If you want a video tutorial on filling these, see ours at our YouTube channel, Cooking with Bruce and Mark.)
4. Generously coat the filled wontons with vegetable oil spray. Set them sealed side up in the air fryer oven with a little room among them. Air-fry undisturbed for 6 minutes, or until golden brown and crisp.
5. Use a nonstick-safe spatula to gently transfer the wontons to a wire rack. Cool for 5 minutes before serving warm.

Crispy Spiced Chickpeas

Servings: 4

Cooking Time: 12 Minutes

Ingredients:

- 1 (15 ounce) can chickpeas, drained, rinsed, and patted dry
- 1 tablespoon olive oil
- ½ teaspoon cumin
- ¼ teaspoon paprika
- ½ teaspoon ground fennel seeds
- ⅛ teaspoon cayenne pepper

Directions:

1. Combine all ingredients in a large bowl and stir to combine.
2. Preheat the toaster oven to 430°F.
3. Place chickpeas on the food tray, then insert the tray at mid position in the preheated oven.
4. Select the Air Fry function, adjust time to 12 minutes, and press Start/Pause.
5. Remove when chickpeas are crispy and golden.

Fried Apple Wedges

Servings: 4

Cooking Time: 9 Minutes

Ingredients:

- ¼ cup panko breadcrumbs
- ¼ cup pecans
- 1½ teaspoons cinnamon
- 1½ teaspoons brown sugar
- ¼ cup cornstarch
- 1 egg white
- 2 teaspoons water
- 1 medium apple
- oil for misting or cooking spray

Directions:

1. In a food processor, combine panko, pecans, cinnamon, and brown sugar. Process to make small crumbs.
2. Place cornstarch in a plastic bag or bowl with lid. In a shallow dish, beat together the egg white and water until slightly foamy.
3. Preheat the toaster oven to 390°F.
4. Cut apple into small wedges. The thickest edge should be no more than ⅜- to ½-inch thick. Cut away the core, but do not peel.
5. Place apple wedges in cornstarch, reseal bag or bowl, and shake to coat.
6. Dip wedges in egg wash, shake off excess, and roll in crumb mixture. Spray with oil.
7. Place apples in air fryer oven in single layer and air-fry for 5 minutes.Break apart any apples that have stuck together. Mist lightly with oil and cook 4 minutes longer, until crispy.

POULTRY

Hot Thighs

Servings: 4

Cooking Time: 40 Minutes

Ingredients:

- 6 skinless, boneless chicken thighs
- ¼ cup fresh lemon juice
- Seasonings:
- 1 teaspoon garlic powder
- ¼ teaspoon cayenne
- ½ teaspoon chili powder
- 1 teaspoon onion powder
- Salt and freshly ground black pepper to taste

Directions:

1. Preheat the toaster oven to 450° F.
2. Brush the chicken thighs liberally with the lemon juice. Set aside.
3. Combine the seasonings in a small bowl and transfer to a paper or plastic bag. Add the thighs and shake well to coat. Remove from the bag and place in an oiled or nonstick 8½ × 8½ × 2-inch square (cake) pan. Cover the pan with aluminum foil.
4. BAKE, covered, for 20 minutes. Turn the pieces with tongs and bake again for another 20 minutes, or until the meat is tender and lightly browned.

Chicken Wellington

Servings: 4

Cooking Time: 30 Minutes

Ingredients:

- 2 small (5- to 6-ounce) boneless, skinless chicken breast halves
- Kosher salt and freshly ground black pepper
- 2 teaspoons Italian seasoning
- 2 tablespoons olive oil
- 3 tablespoons unsalted butter, softened
- 3 ounces cream cheese, softened (about ⅓ cup)
- ¾ cup shredded Monterey Jack cheese
- ¼ cup grated Parmesan cheese
- 1 cup frozen (loose-pack) chopped spinach, thawed and squeezed dry
- ¾ cup chopped canned artichoke hearts, drained
- ½ teaspoon garlic powder
- 1 sheet frozen puff pastry, about 9 inches square, thawed (½ of a 17.3-ounce package)
- 1 large egg, lightly beaten

Directions:

1. Preheat the toaster oven to 425° F. Line a 12 x 12-inch baking pan with parchment paper.
2. Cut the chicken breasts in half lengthwise. Season each piece with the salt, pepper, and Italian seasoning. Fold the thinner end under the larger piece to make the chicken breasts into a rounded shape. Secure with toothpicks.
3. Heat a large skillet over medium-high heat. Add the olive oil and heat. Add the chicken breasts and brown well, turning to brown evenly. Remove from the skillet and set aside to cool. Remove the toothpicks.
4. Stir the butter, cream cheese, Monterey Jack, and Parmesan in a large bowl. Stir in the spinach, artichoke hearts, and garlic powder. Season with salt and pepper.
5. Roll out the puff pastry sheet on a lightly floured board until it makes a 12-inch square. Cut into four equal pieces. Spread one-fourth of the spinach-artichoke mixture on the surface of each pastry square to within ½ inch of all four edges. Place the chicken in the center of each. Gently fold the puff pastry up over the chicken and pinch the edges to seal tightly.
6. Place each chicken bundle, seam side down, on the prepared pan. Brush the top of each bundle lightly with the beaten egg. Bake for 25 to 30 minutes, or until the pastry is golden brown and crisp and a meat thermometer inserted into the chicken reaches 165°F.

Oven-crisped Chicken

Servings: 4

Cooking Time: 35 Minutes

Ingredients:

- Coating mixture:
- 1 cup cornmeal
- ¼ cup wheat germ
- 1 teaspoon paprika
- 1 teaspoon garlic powder
- Salt and butcher's pepper to taste
- 3 tablespoons olive oil
- 1 tablespoon spicy brown mustard
- 6 skinless, boneless chicken thighs

Directions:

1. Preheat the toaster oven to 375° F.
2. Combine the coating mixture ingredients in a small bowl and transfer to a plate, spreading the mixture evenly over the plate's surface. Set aside.
3. Whisk together the oil and mustard in a bowl. Add the chicken pieces and toss to coat thoroughly. Press both sides of each piece into the coating mixture to coat well. Chill in the refrigerator for 10 minutes. Transfer the chicken pieces to a broiling rack with a pan underneath.
4. BAKE, uncovered, for 35 minutes, or until the meat is tender and the coating is crisp and golden brown or browned to your preference.

Honey Lemon Thyme Glazed Cornish Hen

Servings: 2

Cooking Time: 20 Minutes

Ingredients:

- 1 (2-pound) Cornish game hen, split in half
- olive oil
- salt and freshly ground black pepper
- ¼ teaspoon dried thyme
- ¼ cup honey
- 1 tablespoon lemon zest
- juice of 1 lemon
- 1½ teaspoons chopped fresh thyme leaves
- ½ teaspoon soy sauce
- freshly ground black pepper

Directions:

1. Split the game hen in half by cutting down each side of the backbone and then cutting through the breast. Brush or spray both halves of the game hen with the olive oil and then season with the salt, pepper and dried thyme.
2. Preheat the toaster oven to 390°F.
3. Place the game hen, skin side down, into the air fryer oven and air-fry for 5 minutes. Turn the hen halves over and air-fry for 10 minutes.
4. While the hen is cooking, combine the honey, lemon zest and juice, fresh thyme, soy sauce and pepper in a small bowl.
5. When the air fryer oven timer rings, brush the honey glaze onto the game hen and continue to air-fry for another 3 to 5 minutes, just until the hen is nicely glazed, browned and has an internal temperature of 165°F.
6. Let the hen rest for 5 minutes and serve warm.

Italian Roasted Chicken Thighs

Servings: 6

Cooking Time: 14 Minutes

Ingredients:

- 6 boneless chicken thighs
- ½ teaspoon dried oregano
- ½ teaspoon garlic powder
- ½ teaspoon sea salt
- ½ teaspoon black pepper
- ¼ teaspoon crushed red pepper flakes

Directions:

1. Pat the chicken thighs with paper towel.
2. In a small bowl, mix the oregano, garlic powder, salt, pepper, and crushed red pepper flakes. Rub the spice mixture onto the chicken thighs.
3. Preheat the toaster oven to 400°F.
4. Place the chicken thighs in the air fryer oven and spray with cooking spray. Air-fry for 10 minutes, turn over, and cook another 4 minutes. When cooking completes, the internal temperature should read 165°F.

Tandoori Chicken Legs

Servings: 2

Cooking Time: 30 Minutes

Ingredients:

- 1 cup plain yogurt
- 2 cloves garlic, minced
- 1 tablespoon grated fresh ginger
- 2 teaspoons paprika
- 2 teaspoons ground coriander
- 1 teaspoon ground turmeric
- 1 teaspoon salt
- ¼ teaspoon ground cayenne pepper
- juice of 1 lime
- 2 bone-in, skin-on chicken legs
- fresh cilantro leaves

Directions:

1. Make the marinade by combining the yogurt, garlic, ginger, spices and lime juice. Make slashes into the chicken legs to help the marinade penetrate the meat. Pour the marinade over the chicken legs, cover and let the chicken marinate for at least an hour or overnight in the refrigerator.
2. Preheat the toaster oven oven to 380°F.
3. Transfer the chicken legs from the marinade to the air fryer oven, reserving any extra marinade. Air-fry for 15 minutes. Flip the chicken over and pour the remaining marinade over the top. Air-fry for another 15 minutes, watching to make sure it doesn't brown too much. If it does start to get too brown, you can loosely tent the chicken with aluminum foil, tucking the ends of the foil under the chicken to stop it from blowing around.
4. Serve over rice with some fresh cilantro on top.

Crispy Fried Onion Chicken Breasts

Servings: 2

Cooking Time: 13 Minutes

Ingredients:

- ¼ cup all-purpose flour
- salt and freshly ground black pepper
- 1 egg
- 2 tablespoons Dijon mustard
- 1½ cups crispy fried onions (like French's®)
- ½ teaspoon paprika
- 2 (5-ounce) boneless, skinless chicken breasts
- vegetable or olive oil, in a spray bottle

Directions:

1. Preheat the toaster oven to 380°F.
2. Set up a dredging station with three shallow dishes. Place the flour in the first shallow dish and season well with salt and freshly ground black pepper. Combine the egg and Dijon mustard in a second shallow dish and whisk until smooth. Place the fried onions in a sealed bag and using a rolling pin, crush them into coarse crumbs. Combine these crumbs with the paprika in the third shallow dish.
3. Dredge the chicken breasts in the flour. Shake off any excess flour and dip them into the egg mixture. Let any excess egg drip off. Then coat both sides of the chicken breasts with the crispy onions. Press the crumbs onto the chicken breasts with your hands to make sure they are well adhered.
4. Spray or brush the bottom of the air fryer oven with oil. Transfer the chicken breasts to the air fryer oven and air-fry at 380°F for 13 minutes, turning the chicken over halfway through the cooking time.
5. Serve immediately.

Spice-rubbed Split Game Hen

Servings: 2

Cooking Time: 48 Minutes

Ingredients:

- Spice rub mixture:
- 1 teaspoon ground cumin
- 1 teaspoon garlic powder
- 1 teaspoon onion powder
- 1 teaspoon paprika
- 1 teaspoon ground coriander
- 1 teaspoon salt (optional)
- 1 Cornish game hen, split

Directions:

1. Preheat the toaster oven to 400° F.
2. Mix all the spices together in a small bowl and rub each half of the game hen well and on both sides to coat evenly. Place the pieces skin side down in a baking dish. Cover the dish with aluminum foil.
3. BAKE for 20 minutes. Turn the pieces over and bake, covered, for another 20 minutes, or until the meat is tender. Remove from the oven and uncover.
4. BROIL 8 minutes, or until browned to your preference.

Tasty Meat Loaf

Servings: 4

Cooking Time: 35 Minutes

Ingredients:

- 1 to 1½ pounds ground turkey or chicken breast
- 1 egg
- 1 tablespoon chopped fresh parsley
- 2 tablespoons chopped bell pepper
- 3 tablespoons chopped canned mushrooms
- 2 tablespoons chopped onion
- 2 garlic cloves, minced
- ½ cup multigrain bread crumbs
- 1 tablespoon Worcestershire sauce
- 1 tablespoon ketchup
- Freshly ground black pepper to taste

Directions:

1. Preheat the toaster oven to 400° F.
2. Combine all the ingredients in a large bowl and press into a regular-size 4½ × 8½ × 2¼-inch loaf pan.
3. BAKE for 35 minutes, or until browned on top.

Chicken Schnitzel Dogs

Servings: 4

Cooking Time: 10 Minutes

Ingredients:

- ½ cup flour
- ½ teaspoon salt
- 1 teaspoon marjoram
- 1 teaspoon dried parsley flakes
- ½ teaspoon thyme
- 1 egg
- 1 teaspoon lemon juice
- 1 teaspoon water
- 1 cup breadcrumbs
- 4 chicken tenders, pounded thin
- oil for misting or cooking spray
- 4 whole-grain hotdog buns
- 4 slices Gouda cheese
- 1 small Granny Smith apple, thinly sliced
- ½ cup shredded Napa cabbage
- coleslaw dressing

Directions:

1. In a shallow dish, mix together the flour, salt, marjoram, parsley, and thyme.
2. In another shallow dish, beat together egg, lemon juice, and water.
3. Place breadcrumbs in a third shallow dish.
4. Cut each of the flattened chicken tenders in half lengthwise.
5. Dip flattened chicken strips in flour mixture, then egg wash. Let excess egg drip off and roll in breadcrumbs. Spray both sides with oil or cooking spray.
6. Air-fry at 390°F for 5 minutes. Spray with oil, turn over, and spray other side.
7. Air-fry for 3 to 5 minutes more, until well done and crispy brown.
8. To serve, place 2 schnitzel strips on bottom of each hot dog bun. Top with cheese, sliced apple, and cabbage. Drizzle with coleslaw dressing and top with other half of bun.

Chicken Fajitas

Servings: 4

Cooking Time: 15 Minutes

Ingredients:

- FOR THE FAJITAS
- ½ teaspoon ground cumin
- ½ teaspoon garlic powder
- ¼ teaspoon smoked paprika
- ¼ teaspoon onion powder
- ¼ teaspoon chili powder
- 1 pound boneless, skinless chicken breast, cut into ¼-inch strips
- 1 red bell pepper, cut into thin slices
- 1 green bell pepper, cut into thin slices
- 1 small red onion, cut into thin slices
- 2 tablespoons olive oil
- 8 (6-inch) tortillas
- OPTIONAL TOPPINGS
- Salsa
- Sour cream
- Pickled jalapeños
- Shredded lettuce

Directions:

1. Preheat the toaster oven to 375°F on AIR FRY for 5 minutes.
2. Place the air-fryer basket in the baking tray.
3. In a large bowl, stir the cumin, garlic powder, paprika, onion powder, and chili powder until well mixed. Add the chicken, bell peppers, onion, and oil, and toss to coat evenly.
4. Spread the chicken and veggies on the baking sheet.
5. In position 2, air fry for 15 minutes, tossing them halfway through, until cooked and the vegetables are lightly browned.
6. Serve tucked into the tortillas with your favorite toppings.

Parmesan Crusted Chicken Cordon Bleu

Servings: 2

Cooking Time: 14 Minutes

Ingredients:

- 2 (6-ounce) boneless, skinless chicken breasts
- salt and freshly ground black pepper
- 1 tablespoon Dijon mustard
- 4 slices Swiss cheese
- 4 slices deli-sliced ham
- ¼ cup all-purpose flour
- 1 egg, beaten
- ¾ cup panko breadcrumbs
- ⅓ cup grated Parmesan cheese
- olive oil, in a spray bottle

Directions:

1. Butterfly the chicken breasts. Place the chicken breast on a cutting board and press down on the breast with the palm of your hand. Slice into the long side of the chicken breast, parallel to the cutting board, but not all the way through to the other side. Open the chicken breast like a "book". Place a piece of plastic wrap over the chicken breast and gently pound it with a meat mallet to make it evenly thick.
2. Season the chicken with salt and pepper. Spread the Dijon mustard on the inside of each chicken breast. Layer one slice of cheese on top of the mustard, then top with the 2 slices of ham and the other slice of cheese.
3. Starting with the long edge of the chicken breast, roll the chicken up to the other side. Secure it shut with 1 or 2 toothpicks.
4. Preheat the toaster oven to 350°F.
5. Set up a dredging station with three shallow dishes. Place the flour in the first dish. Place the beaten egg in the second shallow dish. Combine the panko breadcrumbs and Parmesan cheese together in the third shallow dish. Dip the stuffed and rolled chicken breasts in the flour, then the beaten egg and then roll in the breadcrumb-cheese mixture to cover on all sides. Press the crumbs onto the chicken breasts with your hands to make sure they are well adhered. Spray the chicken breasts with olive oil and transfer to the air fryer oven.
6. Air-fry at 350°F for 14 minutes, flipping the breasts over halfway through the cooking time. Let the chicken rest for a few minutes before removing the toothpicks, slicing and serving.

BEEF PORK AND LAMB

Albóndigas

Servings: 4

Cooking Time: 15 Minutes

Ingredients:

- 1 pound Lean ground pork
- 3 tablespoons Very finely chopped trimmed scallions
- 3 tablespoons Finely chopped fresh cilantro leaves
- 3 tablespoons Plain panko bread crumbs (gluten-free, if a concern)
- 3 tablespoons Dry white wine, dry sherry, or unsweetened apple juice
- 1½ teaspoons Minced garlic
- 1¼ teaspoons Mild smoked paprika
- ¾ teaspoon Dried oregano
- ¾ teaspoon Table salt
- ¼ teaspoon Ground black pepper
- Olive oil spray

Directions:

1. Preheat the toaster oven to 400°F.
2. Mix the ground pork, scallions, cilantro, bread crumbs, wine or its substitute, garlic, smoked paprika, oregano, salt, and pepper in a bowl until the herbs and spices are evenly distributed in the mixture.
3. Lightly coat your clean hands with olive oil spray, then form the ground pork mixture into balls, using 2 tablespoons for each one. Spray your hands frequently so that the meat mixture doesn't stick.
4. Set the balls in the air fryer oven so that they're not touching, even if they're close together. Air-fry undisturbed for 15 minutes, or until well browned and an instant-read meat thermometer inserted into one or two balls registers 165°F.
5. Use a nonstick-safe spatula and kitchen tongs for balance to gently transfer the fragile balls to a wire rack to cool for 5 minutes before serving.

Orange Glazed Pork Tenderloin

Servings: 3

Cooking Time: 23 Minutes

Ingredients:

- 2 tablespoons brown sugar
- 2 teaspoons cornstarch
- 2 teaspoons Dijon mustard
- ½ cup orange juice
- ½ teaspoon soy sauce
- 2 teaspoons grated fresh ginger
- ¼ cup white wine
- zest of 1 orange
- 1 pound pork tenderloin
- salt and freshly ground black pepper
- oranges, halved (for garnish)
- fresh parsley or other green herb (for garnish)

Directions:

1. Combine the brown sugar, cornstarch, Dijon mustard, orange juice, soy sauce, ginger, white wine and orange zest in a small saucepan and bring the mixture to a boil on the stovetop. Lower the heat and simmer while you cook the pork tenderloin or until the sauce has thickened.
2. Preheat the toaster oven to 370°F.
3. Season all sides of the pork tenderloin with salt and freshly ground black pepper. Transfer the tenderloin to the air fryer oven, bending the pork into a wide "U" shape if necessary to fit in the air fryer oven. Air-fry at 370°F for 20 to 23 minutes, or until the internal temperature reaches 145°F. Flip the tenderloin over halfway through the cooking process and baste with the sauce.
4. Transfer the tenderloin to a cutting board and let it rest for 5 minutes. Slice the pork at a slight angle and serve immediately with orange halves and fresh herbs to dress it up. Drizzle any remaining glaze over the top.

Crispy Smoked Pork Chops

Servings: 3

Cooking Time: 8 Minutes

Ingredients:

- ⅔ cup All-purpose flour or tapioca flour
- 1 Large egg white(s)
- 2 tablespoons Water
- 1½ cups Corn flake crumbs (gluten-free, if a concern)
- 3 ½-pound, ½-inch-thick bone-in smoked pork chops

Directions:

1. Preheat the toaster oven to 375°F.
2. Set up and fill three shallow soup plates or small pie plates on your counter: one for the flour; one for the egg white(s), whisked with the water until foamy; and one for the corn flake crumbs.
3. Set a chop in the flour and turn it several times, coating both sides and the edges. Gently shake off any excess flour, then set it in the beaten egg white mixture. Turn to coat both sides as well as the edges. Let any excess egg white slip back into the rest, then set the chop in the corn flake crumbs. Turn it several times, pressing gently to coat the chop evenly on both sides and around the edge. Set the chop aside and continue coating the remaining chop(s) in the same way.
4. Set the chops in the air fryer oven with as much air space between them as possible. Air-fry undisturbed for 8 minutes, or until the coating is crunchy and the chops are heated through.
5. Use kitchen tongs to transfer the chops to a wire rack and cool for a couple of minutes before serving.

Almond And Sun-dried Tomato Crusted Pork Chops

Servings: 4

Cooking Time: 10 Minutes

Ingredients:

- ½ cup oil-packed sun-dried tomatoes
- ½ cup toasted almonds
- ¼ cup grated Parmesan cheese
- ½ cup olive oil
- 2 tablespoons water
- ½ teaspoon salt
- freshly ground black pepper
- 4 center-cut boneless pork chops (about 1¼ pounds)

Directions:

1. Place the sun-dried tomatoes into a food processor and pulse them until they are coarsely chopped. Add the almonds, Parmesan cheese, olive oil, water, salt and pepper. Process all the ingredients into a smooth paste. Spread most of the paste (leave a little in reserve) onto both sides of the pork chops and then pierce the meat several times with a needle-style meat tenderizer or a fork. Let the pork chops sit and marinate for at least 1 hour (refrigerate if marinating for longer than 1 hour).
2. Preheat the toaster oven to 370°F.
3. Brush a little olive oil on the bottom of the air fryer oven. Transfer the pork chops into the air fryer oven, spooning a little more of the sun-dried tomato paste onto the pork chops if there are any gaps where the paste may have been rubbed off. Air-fry the pork chops at 370°F for 10 minutes, turning the chops over halfway through the cooking process.
4. When the pork chops have finished cooking, transfer them to a serving plate and serve with mashed potatoes and vegetables for a hearty meal.

Extra Crispy Country-style Pork Riblets

Servings: 3

Cooking Time: 30 Minutes

Ingredients:

- ⅓ cup Tapioca flour
- 2½ tablespoons Chile powder
- ¾ teaspoon Table salt (optional)
- 1¼ pounds Boneless country-style pork ribs, cut into 1½-inch chunks
- Vegetable oil spray

Directions:

1. Preheat the toaster oven to 375°F .
2. Mix the tapioca flour, chile powder, and salt (if using) in a large bowl until well combined. Add the country-style rib chunks and toss well to coat thoroughly.
3. When the machine is at temperature, gently shake off any excess tapioca coating from the chunks. Generously coat them on all sides with vegetable oil spray. Arrange the chunks in the air fryer oven in one (admittedly fairly tight) layer. The pieces may touch. Air-fry for 30 minutes, rearranging the pieces at the 10- and 20-minute marks to expose any touching bits, until very crisp and well browned.
4. Gently pour the contents of the pan onto a wire rack. Cool for 5 minutes before serving.

Italian Sausage & Peppers

Servings: 6

Cooking Time: 25 Minutes

Ingredients:

- 1 6-ounce can tomato paste
- ⅔ cup water
- 1 8-ounce can tomato sauce
- 1 teaspoon dried parsley flakes
- ½ teaspoon garlic powder
- ⅛ teaspoon oregano
- ½ pound mild Italian bulk sausage
- 1 tablespoon extra virgin olive oil
- ½ large onion, cut in 1-inch chunks
- 4 ounces fresh mushrooms, sliced
- 1 large green bell pepper, cut in 1-inch chunks
- 8 ounces spaghetti, cooked
- Parmesan cheese for serving

Directions:

1. In a large saucepan or skillet, stir together the tomato paste, water, tomato sauce, parsley, garlic, and oregano. Heat on stovetop over very low heat while preparing meat and vegetables.
2. Break sausage into small chunks, about ½-inch pieces. Place in air fryer oven baking pan.
3. Air-fry at 390°F for 5 minutes. Stir. Cook 7 minutes longer or until sausage is well done. Remove from pan, drain on paper towels, and add to the sauce mixture.
4. If any sausage grease remains in baking pan, pour it off or use paper towels to soak it up. (Be careful handling that hot pan!)
5. Place olive oil, onions, and mushrooms in pan and stir. Air-fry for 5 minutes or just until tender. Using a slotted spoon, transfer onions and mushrooms from baking pan into the sauce and sausage mixture.
6. Place bell pepper chunks in air fryer oven baking pan and air-fry for 8 minutes or until tender. When done, stir into sauce with sausage and other vegetables.
7. Serve over cooked spaghetti with plenty of Parmesan cheese.

Red Curry Flank Steak

Servings: 4

Cooking Time: 18 Minutes

Ingredients:

- 3 tablespoons red curry paste
- ¼ cup olive oil
- 2 teaspoons grated fresh ginger
- 2 tablespoons soy sauce
- 2 tablespoons rice wine vinegar
- 3 scallions, minced
- 1½ pounds flank steak
- fresh cilantro (or parsley) leaves

Directions:

1. Mix the red curry paste, olive oil, ginger, soy sauce, rice vinegar and scallions together in a bowl. Place the flank steak in a shallow glass dish and pour half the marinade over the steak. Pierce the steak several times with a fork or meat tenderizer to let the marinade penetrate the meat. Turn the steak over, pour the remaining marinade over the top and pierce the steak several times again. Cover and marinate the steak in the refrigerator for 6 to 8 hours.
2. When you are ready to cook, remove the steak from the refrigerator and let it sit at room temperature for 30 minutes.
3. Preheat the toaster oven to 400°F.
4. Cut the flank steak in half so that it fits more easily into the air fryer oven and transfer both pieces to the air fryer oven. Pour the marinade over the steak. Air-fry for 18 minutes, depending on your preferred degree of doneness of the steak (12 minutes = medium rare). Flip the steak over halfway through the cooking time.
5. When your desired degree of doneness has been reached, remove the steak to a cutting board and let it rest for 5 minutes before slicing. Thinly slice the flank steak against the grain of the meat. Transfer the slices to a serving platter, pour any juice from the bottom of the air fryer oven over the sliced flank steak and sprinkle the fresh cilantro on top.

Classic Pepperoni Pizza

Servings: 4

Cooking Time: 11 Minutes

Ingredients:

- Oil spray (hand-pumped)
- 1 pound premade pizza dough, or your favorite recipe
- ½ cup store-bought pizza sauce
- ¼ cup grated Parmesan cheese
- ¾ cup shredded mozzarella
- 10 to 12 slices pepperoni
- 2 tablespoons chopped fresh basil
- Pinch red pepper flakes

Directions:

1. Preheat the toaster oven to 425°F on BAKE for 5 minutes.
2. Spray the baking tray with the oil and spread the pizza dough with your fingertips so that it covers the tray. Prick the dough with a fork.
3. In position 2, bake for 8 minutes until the crust is lightly golden.
4. Take the crust out and spread with the pizza sauce, leaving a ½-inch border around the edge. Sprinkle with Parmesan and mozzarella cheeses and arrange the pepperoni on the pizza.
5. Bake for 3 minutes until the cheese is melted and bubbly.
6. Top with the basil and red pepper flakes and serve.

Chinese Pork And Vegetable Non-stir-fry

Servings: 4

Cooking Time: 30 Minutes

Ingredients:

- Seasoning sauce:
- 1 tablespoon soy sauce
- ¼ cup dry white wine
- 1 tablespoon sesame oil
- 1 tablespoon vegetable oil
- 1 teaspoon Chinese five-spice powder
- 2 6-ounce lean boneless pork chops cut into ¼ × 2-inch strips
- 1 1-pound package frozen vegetable mix or 2 cups sliced assorted fresh vegetables: broccoli, carrots, cauliflower, bell pepper, and the like
- 1 4-ounce can mushroom pieces, drained, or ½ cup cleaned and sliced fresh mushrooms
- 2 tablespoons sesame seeds
- 2 tablespoons minced fresh garlic

Directions:

1. Whisk together the seasoning sauce ingredients in a small bowl. Set aside.
2. Combine the pork, vegetables, mushrooms, sesame seeds, and garlic in an oiled or nonstick 8½ × 8½ × 2-inch square baking (cake) pan. Add the seasoning sauce ingredients and toss to coat the pork, vegetables, and mushrooms well.
3. BROIL for 30 minutes, turning with tongs every 8 minutes, until the vegetables and meat are well cooked and lightly browned.

Better-than-chinese-take-out Pork Ribs

Servings: 3

Cooking Time: 35 Minutes

Ingredients:

- 1½ tablespoons Hoisin sauce (gluten-free, if a concern)
- 1½ tablespoons Regular or low-sodium soy sauce or gluten-free tamari sauce
- 1½ tablespoons Shaoxing (Chinese cooking rice wine), dry sherry, or white grape juice
- 1½ teaspoons Minced garlic
- ¾ teaspoon Ground dried ginger
- ¾ teaspoon Ground white pepper
- 1½ pounds Pork baby back rib rack(s), cut into 2-bone pieces

Directions:

1. Mix the hoisin sauce, soy or tamari sauce, Shaoxing or its substitute, garlic, ginger, and white pepper in a large bowl. Add the rib sections and stir well to coat. Cover and refrigerate for at least 2 hours or up to 24 hours, stirring the rib sections in the marinade occasionally.
2. Preheat the toaster oven to 350°F . Set the ribs in their bowl on the counter as the machine heats.
3. When the machine is at temperature, set the rib pieces on their sides in a single layer in the air fryer oven with as much air space between them as possible. Air-fry for 35 minutes, turning and rearranging the pieces once, until deeply browned and sizzling.
4. Use kitchen tongs to transfer the rib pieces to a large serving bowl or platter. Wait a minute or two before serving them so the meat can reabsorb some of its own juices.

Kielbasa Chunks With Pineapple & Peppers

Servings: 2

Cooking Time: 10 Minutes

Ingredients:

- ¾ pound kielbasa sausage
- 1 cup bell pepper chunks (any color)
- 1 8-ounce can pineapple chunks in juice, drained
- 1 tablespoon barbeque seasoning
- 1 tablespoon soy sauce
- cooking spray

Directions:

1. Cut sausage into ½-inch slices.
2. In a medium bowl, toss all ingredients together.
3. Spray air fryer oven with nonstick cooking spray.
4. Pour sausage mixture into the air fryer oven.
5. Air-fry at 390°F for approximately 5 minutes. Cook an additional 5 minutes.

Chicken Fried Steak

Servings: 4

Cooking Time: 15 Minutes

Ingredients:

- 2 eggs
- ½ cup buttermilk
- 1½ cups flour
- ¾ teaspoon salt
- ½ teaspoon pepper
- 1 pound beef cube steaks
- salt and pepper
- oil for misting or cooking spray

Directions:

1. Beat together eggs and buttermilk in a shallow dish.
2. In another shallow dish, stir together the flour, ½ teaspoon salt, and ¼ teaspoon pepper.
3. Season cube steaks with remaining salt and pepper to taste. Dip in flour, buttermilk egg wash, and then flour again.
4. Spray both sides of steaks with oil or cooking spray.
5. Cooking in 2 batches, place steaks in air fryer oven in single layer. Air-fry at 360°F for 10 minutes. Spray tops of steaks with oil and cook 5 minutes or until meat is well done.
6. Repeat to cook remaining steaks.

VEGETABLES AND VEGETARIAN

Roasted Veggie Kebabs

Servings: 4

Cooking Time: 45 Minutes

Ingredients:

- Brushing mixture:
- 3 tablespoons olive oil
- 1 tablespoon soy sauce
- 1 teaspoon garlic powder
- 1 teaspoon ground cumin
- 2 tablespoons balsamic vinegar
- Salt and freshly ground black pepper to taste
- Cauliflower, zucchini, onion, broccoli, bell pepper, mushrooms, celery, cabbage, beets, and the like, cut into approximately 2 × 2-inch pieces

Directions:

1. Preheat the toaster oven to 400° F.
2. Combine the brushing mixture ingredients in a small bowl, mixing well. Set aside.
3. Skewer the vegetable pieces on 4 9-inch metal skewers and place the skewers lengthwise on a broiling rack with a pan underneath.
4. BAKE for 40 minutes, or until the vegetables are tender, brushing with the mixture every 10 minutes.
5. BROIL for 5 minutes, or until lightly browned.

Rosemary New Potatoes

Servings: 4

Cooking Time: 6 Minutes

Ingredients:

- 3 large red potatoes (enough to make 3 cups sliced)
- ¼ teaspoon ground rosemary
- ¼ teaspoon ground thyme
- ⅛ teaspoon salt
- ⅛ teaspoon ground black pepper
- 2 teaspoons extra-light olive oil

Directions:

1. Preheat the toaster oven to 330°F.
2. Place potatoes in large bowl and sprinkle with rosemary, thyme, salt, and pepper.
3. Stir with a spoon to distribute seasonings evenly.
4. Add oil to potatoes and stir again to coat well.
5. Air-fry at 330°F for 4 minutes. Stir and break apart any that have stuck together.
6. Cook an additional 2 minutes or until fork-tender.

Sweet Potato Curly Fries

Servings: 4

Cooking Time: 10 Minutes

Ingredients:

- 2 medium sweet potatoes, washed
- 2 tablespoons avocado oil
- ¾ teaspoon salt, divided
- 1 medium avocado
- ½ teaspoon garlic powder
- ½ teaspoon paprika
- ¼ teaspoon black pepper
- ½ juice lime
- 3 tablespoons fresh cilantro

Directions:

1. Preheat the toaster oven to 400°F.
2. Using a spiralizer, create curly spirals with the sweet potatoes. Keep the pieces about 1½ inches long. Continue until all the potatoes are used.
3. In a large bowl, toss the curly sweet potatoes with the avocado oil and ½ teaspoon of the salt.
4. Place the potatoes in the air fryer oven and air-fry for 5 minutes; cook another 5 minutes.
5. While cooking, add the avocado, garlic, paprika, pepper, the remaining ¼ teaspoon of salt, lime juice, and cilantro to a blender and process until smooth. Set aside.
6. When cooking completes, remove the fries and serve warm with the lime avocado sauce.

Mini Hasselback Potatoes

Servings: 25

Cooking Time: 4 Minutes

Ingredients:

- 1½ pounds baby Yukon Gold potatoes (about 10)
- 5 tablespoons butter, cut into very thin slices
- salt and freshly ground black pepper
- 1 tablespoon vegetable oil
- ¼ cup grated Parmesan cheese (optional)
- chopped fresh parsley or chives

Directions:

1. Preheat the toaster oven to 400°F.
2. Make six to eight deep vertical slits across the top of each potato about three quarters of the way down. Make sure the slits are deep enough to allow the slices to spread apart a little, but don't cut all the way through the potato. Place a thin slice of butter between each of the slices and season generously with salt and pepper.
3. Transfer the potatoes to the air fryer oven. Pack them in next to each other. It's alright if some of the potatoes sit on top or rest on another potato. Air-fry for 20 minutes.
4. Spray or brush the potatoes with a little vegetable oil and sprinkle the Parmesan cheese on top. Air-fry for an additional 5 minutes. Garnish with chopped parsley or chives and serve hot.

Mashed Potato Tots

Servings: 18

Cooking Time: 10 Minutes

Ingredients:

- 1 medium potato or 1 cup cooked mashed potatoes
- 1 tablespoon real bacon bits
- 2 tablespoons chopped green onions, tops only
- ¼ teaspoon onion powder
- 1 teaspoon dried chopped chives
- salt
- 2 tablespoons flour
- 1 egg white, beaten
- ½ cup panko breadcrumbs
- oil for misting or cooking spray

Directions:

1. If using cooked mashed potatoes, jump to step 4.
2. Peel potato and cut into ½-inch cubes. (Small pieces cook more quickly.) Place in saucepan, add water to cover, and heat to boil. Lower heat slightly and continue cooking just until tender, about 10 minutes.
3. Drain potatoes and place in ice cold water. Allow to cool for a minute or two, then drain well and mash.
4. Preheat the toaster oven to 390°F.
5. In a large bowl, mix together the potatoes, bacon bits, onions, onion powder, chives, salt to taste, and flour. Add egg white and stir well.
6. Place panko crumbs on a sheet of wax paper.
7. For each tot, use about 2 teaspoons of potato mixture. To shape, drop the measure of potato mixture onto panko crumbs and push crumbs up and around potatoes to coat edges. Then turn tot over to coat other side with crumbs.
8. Mist tots with oil or cooking spray and place in air fryer oven, crowded but not stacked.
9. Air-fry at 390°F for 10 minutes, until browned and crispy.
10. Repeat steps 8 and 9 to cook remaining tots.

Grits Again

Servings: 2

Cooking Time: 10 Minutes

Ingredients:

- cooked grits
- plain breadcrumbs
- oil for misting or cooking spray
- honey or maple syrup for serving (optional)

Directions:

1. While grits are still warm, spread them into a square or rectangular baking pan, about ½-inch thick. If your grits are thicker than that, scoop some out into another pan.
2. Chill several hours or overnight, until grits are cold and firm.
3. When ready to cook, pour off any water that has collected in pan and cut grits into 2- to 3-inch squares.
4. Dip grits squares in breadcrumbs and place in air fryer oven in single layer, close but not touching.
5. Air-fry at 390°F for 10 minutes, until heated through and crispy brown on the outside.
6. Serve while hot either plain or with a drizzle of honey or maple syrup.

Steakhouse Baked Potatoes

Servings: 3

Cooking Time: 55 Minutes

Ingredients:

- 3 10-ounce russet potatoes
- 2 tablespoons Olive oil
- 1 teaspoon Table salt

Directions:

1. Preheat the toaster oven to 375°F .
2. Poke holes all over each potato with a fork. Rub the skin of each potato with 2 teaspoons of the olive oil, then sprinkle ¼ teaspoon salt all over each potato.
3. When the machine is at temperature, set the potatoes in the air fryer oven in one layer with as much air space between them as possible. Air-fry for 50 minutes, turning once, or until soft to the touch but with crunchy skins. If the machine is at 360°F, you may need to add up to 5 minutes to the cooking time.
4. Use kitchen tongs to gently transfer the baked potatoes to a wire rack. Cool for 5 or 10 minutes before serving.

Crispy Brussels Sprouts

Servings: 3

Cooking Time: 12 Minutes

Ingredients:

- 1¼ pounds Medium, 2-inch-in-length Brussels sprouts
- 1½ tablespoons Olive oil
- ¾ teaspoon Table salt

Directions:

1. Preheat the toaster oven to 400°F.
2. Halve each Brussels sprout through the stem end, pulling off and discarding any discolored outer leaves. Put the sprout halves in a large bowl, add the oil and salt, and stir well to coat evenly, until the Brussels sprouts are glistening.
3. When the machine is at temperature, scrape the contents of the bowl into the air fryer oven, gently spreading the Brussels sprout halves into as close to one layer as possible. Air-fry for 12 minutes, gently tossing and rearranging the vegetables twice to get all covered or touching parts exposed to the air currents, until crisp and browned at the edges.
4. Gently pour the contents of the air fryer oven onto a wire rack. Cool for a minute or two before serving.

Fried Green Tomatoes With Sriracha Mayo

Servings: 4

Cooking Time: 12 Minutes

Ingredients:

- 3 green tomatoes
- salt and freshly ground black pepper
- ⅓ cup all-purpose flour
- 2 eggs
- ½ cup buttermilk
- 1 cup panko breadcrumbs
- 1 cup cornmeal
- olive oil, in a spray bottle
- fresh thyme sprigs or chopped fresh chives
- Sriracha Mayo
- ½ cup mayonnaise
- 1 to 2 tablespoons sriracha hot sauce
- 1 tablespoon milk

Directions:

1. Cut the tomatoes in ¼-inch slices. Pat them dry with a clean kitchen towel and season generously with salt and pepper.
2. Set up a dredging station using three shallow dishes. Place the flour in the first shallow dish, whisk the eggs and buttermilk together in the second dish, and combine the panko breadcrumbs and cornmeal in the third dish.
3. Preheat the toaster oven to 400°F.
4. Dredge the tomato slices in flour to coat on all sides. Then dip them into the egg mixture and finally press them into the breadcrumbs to coat all sides of the tomato.
5. Spray or brush the air-fryer oven with olive oil. Transfer 3 to 4 tomato slices into the air fryer oven and spray the top with olive oil. Air-fry the tomatoes at 400°F for 8 minutes. Flip them over, spray the other side with oil and air-fry for an additional 4 minutes until golden brown.
6. While the tomatoes are cooking, make the sriracha mayo. Combine the mayonnaise, 1 tablespoon of the sriracha hot sauce and milk in a small bowl. Stir well until the mixture is smooth. Add more sriracha sauce to taste.
7. When the tomatoes are done, transfer them to a cooling rack or a platter lined with paper towels so the bottom does not get soggy. Before serving, carefully stack the all the tomatoes into air fryer oven and air-fry at 350°F for 1 to 2 minutes to heat them back up.
8. Serve the fried green tomatoes hot with the sriracha mayo on the side. Season one last time with salt and freshly ground black pepper and garnish with sprigs of fresh thyme or chopped fresh chives.

Roasted Fennel Salad

Servings: 3

Cooking Time: 20 Minutes

Ingredients:

- 3 cups (about ¾ pound) Trimmed fennel, roughly chopped
- 1½ tablespoons Olive oil
- ¼ teaspoon Table salt
- ¼ teaspoon Ground black pepper
- 1½ tablespoons White balsamic vinegar

Directions:

1. Preheat the toaster oven to 400°F.
2. Toss the fennel, olive oil, salt, and pepper in a large bowl until the fennel is well coated in the oil.
3. When the machine is at temperature, pour the fennel into the air fryer oven, spreading it out into as close to one layer as possible. Air-fry for 20 minutes, tossing and rearranging the fennel pieces twice so that any covered or touching parts get exposed to the air currents, until golden at the edges and softened.
4. Pour the fennel into a serving bowl. Add the vinegar while hot. Toss well, then cool a couple of minutes before serving. Or serve at room temperature.

Latkes

Servings: 12

Cooking Time: 13 Minutes

Ingredients:

- 1 russet potato
- ¼ onion
- 2 eggs, lightly beaten
- ⅓ cup flour
- ½ teaspoon baking powder
- 1 teaspoon salt
- freshly ground black pepper
- canola or vegetable oil, in a spray bottle
- chopped chives, for garnish
- apple sauce
- sour cream

Directions:

1. Shred the potato and onion with a coarse box grater or a food processor with the shredding blade. Place the shredded vegetables into a colander or mesh strainer and squeeze or press down firmly to remove the excess water.
2. Transfer the onion and potato to a large bowl and add the eggs, flour, baking powder, salt and black pepper. Mix to combine and then shape the mixture into patties, about ¼-cup of mixture each. Brush or spray both sides of the latkes with oil.
3. Preheat the toaster oven to 400°F.
4. Air-fry the latkes in batches. Transfer one layer of the latkes to the air fryer oven and air-fry at 400°F for 12 to 13 minutes, flipping them over halfway through the cooking time. Transfer the finished latkes to a platter and cover with aluminum foil, or place them in a warm oven to keep warm.
5. Garnish the latkes with chopped chives and serve with sour cream and applesauce.

Zucchini Fries

Servings: 3

Cooking Time: 12 Minutes

Ingredients:

- 1 large Zucchini
- ½ cup All-purpose flour or tapioca flour
- 2 Large egg(s), well beaten
- 1 cup Seasoned Italian-style dried bread crumbs (gluten-free, if a concern)
- Olive oil spray

Directions:

1. Preheat the toaster oven to 400°F.
2. Trim the zucchini into a long rectangular block, taking off the ends and four "sides" to make this shape. Cut the block lengthwise into ½-inch-thick slices. Lay these slices flat and cut in half widthwise. Slice each of these pieces into ½-inch-thick batons.
3. Set up and fill three shallow soup plates or small pie plates on your counter: one for the flour, one for the beaten egg(s), and one for the bread crumbs.
4. Set a zucchini baton in the flour and turn it several times to coat all sides. Gently stir any excess flour, then dip it in the egg(s), turning it to coat. Let any excess egg slip back into the rest, then set the baton in the bread crumbs and turn it several times, pressing gently to coat all sides, even the ends. Set aside on a cutting board and continue coating the remainder of the batons in the same way.
5. Lightly coat the batons on all sides with olive oil spray. Set them in two flat layers in the air fryer oven, the top layer at a 90-degree angle to the bottom one, with a little air space between the batons in each layer. In the end, the whole thing will look like a crosshatch pattern. Air-fry undisturbed for 6 minutes.
6. Use kitchen tongs to gently rearrange the batons so that any covered parts are now uncovered. The batons no longer need to be in a crosshatch pattern. Continue air-frying undisturbed for 6 minutes, or until lightly browned and crisp.
7. Gently pour the contents of the air fryer oven onto a wire rack. Spread the batons out and cool for only a minute or two before serving.

LUNCH AND DINNER

Parmesan Artichoke Pizza

Servings: 6 Cooking Time: 15 Minutes

Ingredients:

- CRUST
- ¾ cup warm water (110°F)
- 1 ½ teaspoons active dry yeast
- ¼ teaspoon sugar
- 1 tablespoon olive oil
- 1 teaspoon table salt
- ⅓ cup whole wheat flour
- 1 ½ to 1 ⅔ cups bread flour
- TOPPINGS
- 2 tablespoons olive oil
- 1 teaspoon Italian seasoning
- 1 clove garlic, minced
- ½ cup whole milk ricotta cheese, at room temperature
- ⅔ cup drained, chopped marinated artichokes
- ¼ cup chopped red onion
- 3 tablespoons minced fresh basil
- ½ cup shredded Parmesan cheese
- ⅓ cup shredded mozzarella cheese

Directions:

1. Make the Crust: Place the warm water, yeast, and sugar in a large mixing bowl for a stand mixer. Stir, then let stand for 3 to 5 minutes or until bubbly.
2. Stir in the olive oil, salt, whole wheat flour, and 1 ½ cups bread flour. If the dough is too sticky, stir in an additional 1 to 2 tablespoons bread flour. Beat with the flat (paddle) beater at medium-speed for 5 minutes (or knead by hand for 5 to 7 minutes or until the dough is smooth and elastic). Place in a greased large bowl, turn the dough over, cover with a clean towel, and let stand for 30 to 45 minutes, or until starting to rise.
3. Stir the olive oil, Italian seasoning, and garlic in a small bowl; set aside.
4. Preheat the toaster oven to 450°F. Place a 12-inch pizza pan in the toaster oven while it is preheating.
5. Turn the dough onto a lightly floured surface and pull or roll the dough to make a 12-inch circle. Carefully transfer the crust to the hot pan.
6. Brush the olive oil mixture over the crust. Spread the ricotta evenly over the crust. Top with the artichokes, red onions, fresh basil, Parmesan, and mozzarella. Bake for 13 to 15 minutes, or until the crust is golden brown and the cheese is melted. Let stand for 5 minutes before cutting.

Chicken Gumbo

Servings: 4

Cooking Time: 40 Minutes

Ingredients:

- 2 skinless, boneless chicken breast halves, cut into 1-inch cubes
- ½ cup dry red wine
- 1 small onion, finely chopped
- 1 celery stalk, finely chopped
- 2 plum tomatoes, chopped
- 3 1 bell pepper, chopped
- 1 tablespoon minced fresh garlic
- 2 okra pods, stemmed, seeded, and finely chopped 1 bay leaf
- ½ teaspoon hot sauce
- ½ teaspoon dried thyme
- Salt and freshly ground black pepper to taste

Directions:

1. Preheat the toaster oven to 400° F.
2. Combine all the ingredients in a 1-quart 8½ × 8½ × 4-inch ovenproof baking dish. Adjust the seasonings to taste. Cover with aluminum foil.
3. BAKE, covered, for 40 minutes, or until the onion, pepper, and celery are tender. Discard the bay leaf before serving.

Pesto Pizza

Servings: 1

Cooking Time: 20 Minutes

Ingredients:

- Topping:
- ½ cup chopped fresh basil
- 1 tablespoon pine nuts (pignoli)
- 1 tablespoon olive oil
- 2 tablespoons shredded Parmesan cheese
- 1 garlic clove, minced
- ½ teaspoon dried oregano or 1 tablespoon chopped fresh oregano
- 1 plum tomato, chopped
- Salt and pepper to taste
- 1 9-inch ready-made pizza crust
- 2 tablespoons shredded low-fat mozzarella

Directions:

1. Preheat the toaster oven to 375° F.
2. Combine the topping ingredients in a small bowl.
3. Process the mixture in a blender or food processor until smooth. Spread the mixture on the pizza crust, then sprinkle with the mozzarella cheese. Place the pizza crust on the toaster oven rack.
4. BAKE for 20 minutes, or until the cheese is melted and the crust is brown.

Roasted Harissa Chicken + Vegetables

Servings: 4

Cooking Time: 30 Minutes

Ingredients:

- Nonstick cooking spray
- 1 medium zucchini, halved lengthwise and sliced crosswise ½ inch thick
- ½ large red onion, sliced ¼ inch thick
- 2 tablespoons olive oil
- Kosher salt and freshly ground black pepper
- 1 pound boneless, skinless chicken breasts, cut into 1-inch cubes
- ½ teaspoon ground cumin
- 1 clove garlic, minced
- 2 tablespoons harissa sauce or paste
- 1 tablespoon honey
- 2 tablespoons minced fresh cilantro
- 2 cups hot cooked rice
- Optional toppings: plain Greek yogurt or sour cream, sesame seeds (toasted or chopped), or dry-roasted peanuts

Directions:

1. Preheat the toaster oven to 400°F. Spray a 12 x 12-inch baking pan with nonstick cooking spray.
2. Place the zucchini and red onion in a medium bowl. Drizzle with 1 tablespoon olive oil and season with salt and pepper. Stir to coat the vegetables evenly. Arrange the vegetables in a single layer in the prepared baking pan. Roast, uncovered, for 10 minutes.
3. Place the chicken cubes in that same bowl. Drizzle with the remaining 1 tablespoon olive oil. Season with the cumin, garlic, salt, and pepper. Stir to coat the chicken evenly.
4. Stir the vegetables and move to one side of the pan. Arrange the chicken in a single layer on the other side of the pan. Roast for 10 minutes.
5. Blend the harissa and honey in a small bowl. Drizzle the sauce over the chicken and vegetables. Using a pastry brush, coat the chicken and vegetables evenly. Roast, uncovered, for an additional 8 to 10 minutes, or until the vegetables are tender and the chicken registers 165°F on a meat thermometer.
6. Spoon the chicken, vegetables, and any collected liquid onto a serving platter. Sprinkle with the cilantro. Serve the chicken and vegetables with the rice and, if desired, a dollop of plain Greek yogurt and a sprinkling of sesame seeds.

Chicken Marengo

Servings: 4

Cooking Time: 30 Minutes

Ingredients:

- Chicken mixture:
- 2 skinless, boneless chicken breast halves, cut into 1 × 1-inch pieces
- 6 large shrimp, peeled, deveined, and cut into 1 × 1-inch pieces
- 2 plum tomatoes, chopped
- 1 tablespoon olive oil
- ½ cup dry white wine
- 3 garlic cloves, chopped
- 6 fresh mushrooms, rinsed quickly, patted dry, and thinly sliced
- 1 teaspoon dried tarragon
- 1 tablespoon chopped fresh parsley
- Salt and freshly ground black pepper to taste
- 2 hard-boiled eggs, peeled and sliced
- ½ cup pitted and sliced black olives
- 2 tablespoons chopped fresh parsley

Directions:

1. Preheat the toaster oven to 375° F.
2. Combine the chicken mixture ingredients in a 1-quart 8½ × 8½ × 4-inch ovenproof baking dish and adjust the seasonings to taste. Cover with aluminum foil.
3. BAKE, covered, for 30 minutes, or until the chicken and shrimp are tender.
4. Garnish with slices of hard-boiled eggs, black olives, and parsley.

Thai Chicken Pizza With Cauliflower Crust

Servings: 6 Cooking Time: 20 Minutes

Ingredients:

- Nonstick cooking spray
- ½ large head cauliflower (about 1 pound), cut into florets (3 ½ to 4 cups)
- 2 large eggs, lightly beaten
- ⅓ cup shredded mozzarella cheese
- 3 tablespoons shredded Parmesan cheese
- 2 teaspoons Italian seasoning
- ½ teaspoon garlic powder
- Kosher salt and freshly ground black pepper
- SAUCE
- ¼ cup creamy peanut butter
- 1 ½ tablespoons reduced-sodium soy sauce
- 1 ½ tablespoons fresh lime juice
- 1 tablespoon honey
- 1 tablespoon unseasoned rice vinegar
- ½ teaspoon chili garlic sauce
- TOPPINGS
- 1 cup chopped or shredded cooked chicken
- 1 carrot, shredded
- 2 green onions, white and green portions, thinly sliced
- 1 cup shredded Monterey Jack cheese

Directions:

1. Preheat the toaster oven to 425°F. Line a 12-inch pizza pan with parchment paper. Spray with nonstick cooking spray.
2. Place the cauliflower in the work bowl of a food processor. Pulse until finely chopped. (Work in batches, as necessary, so as not to overload the food processor.) Transfer the cauliflower rice to a large, microwave-safe bowl. Add 1 tablespoon water. Cover and microwave on High (100 percent) power for 3 minutes or until the cauliflower is tender. Uncover and let the cauliflower cool to room temperature.
3. Spoon the cauliflower into a clean kitchen towel and twist to drain the cauliflower well. Return the drained cauliflower to the bowl. Stir in the eggs, mozzarella, Parmesan, Italian seasoning, and garlic powder and season with salt and pepper. Stir well.
4. Spoon the cauliflower mixture onto the prepared pan. Gently spread or pat the mixture into an even circle, about 11 inches in diameter. Bake for 12 to 15 minutes or until the crust is set and beginning to brown.
5. Meanwhile, make the sauce: Stir the peanut butter, soy sauce, lime juice, honey, vinegar, and chili garlic sauce in a small bowl.
6. Remove the cauliflower crust from the toaster oven. Spread the peanut sauce over the crust. Top with the chicken, carrot, green onions, and Monterey Jack cheese. Bake for 5 minutes or until hot and the cheese is melted.

Narragansett Clam Chowder

Servings: 4

Cooking Time: 35 Minutes

Ingredients:

- 1 cup fat-free half-and-half
- 2 tablespoons unbleached flour
- 3 ½ cup chopped onion
- 1 cup peeled and diced potato
- 1 tablespoon vegetable oil
- 1 tablespoon chopped fresh parsley
- 1 6-ounce can clams, drained and chopped
- 1 15-ounce can fat-free low-sodium chicken broth
- Salt and freshly ground black pepper

Directions:

1. Whisk together the half-and-half and flour in a small bowl. Set aside.
2. Combine the onion, potato, and oil in an 8½ × 8½ × 2-inch square baking (cake) pan.
3. BROIL 15 minutes, turning every 5 minutes with tongs, or until the potato is tender and the onion is cooked. Transfer to a 1-quart baking dish. Add the parsley, clams, broth, and half-and-half/flour mixture. Stir well and season to taste with salt and pepper.
4. BAKE, uncovered, at 375° F. for 20 minutes, stirring after 10 minutes, or until the stock is reduced and thickened. Ladle into bowls and serve with Yogurt Bread.

Meat Lovers Pan Pizza

Servings: 9

Cooking Time: 15 Minutes

Ingredients:

- Dough
- ¾ cup plus 1½ tablespoons warm water, 100°-110°F
- 1¾ teaspoons instant yeast
- 2 cups all-purpose flour, plus more for dusting
- 1 teaspoon kosher salt
- 1 tablespoon extra virgin olive oil, plus more for drizzling
- Toppings
- 6 tablespoons pizza sauce
- 8 ounces shredded low-moisture mozzarella
- Pepperoni slices
- 8 ounces cooked Italian sausage
- Crushed red pepper, for sprinkling
- Dried oregano, for sprinkling
- Black pepper, for sprinkling

Directions:

1. Pour water into a large mixing bowl, then whisk in the yeast. Allow to bloom for 10 minutes.
2. Add the flour and salt and mix with your hands until no dry flour remains.
3. Cover the dough tightly with plastic wrap and allow to rest at room temperature for 15 hours.
4. Add the olive oil and form into a ball.
5. Drizzle extra-virgin olive oil generously on the food tray and use your hands to coat evenly.
6. Place the dough on the food tray and spread it out slightly toward the corners of the pan.
7. Drizzle some more extra-virgin olive oil on top and use your hands to evenly coat the top of the dough.
8. Cover the dough and allow it to rest for 90 minutes.
9. Spread the dough out further so that it covers the bottom of the pan, then pop any bubbles that formed in the dough.
10. Spread pizza sauce on the dough, followed by cheese, then pepperoni and sausage.
11. Sprinkle the pizza with crushed red pepper, dried oregano, and black pepper.
12. Preheat the toaster Oven to 450°F.
13. Insert the pizza at low position in the preheated oven.
14. Select the Pizza function, adjust time to 15 minutes, and press Start/Pause.
15. Remove when done and allow to rest for 5 minutes before cutting.
16. Cut the pizza into squares and serve.

Spanako Pizza

Servings: 2

Cooking Time: 30 Minutes

Ingredients:

- 8 sheets phyllo dough, thawed and folded in half
- 4 tablespoons olive oil
- 4 tablespoons grated Parmesan cheese
- Topping mixture:
- 1 10-ounce package frozen chopped spinach, thawed and well drained
- 1 plum tomato, finely chopped
- ¼ cup finely chopped onion
- ¼ cup shredded low-fat mozzarella cheese
- 3 tablespoons crumbled feta cheese or part-skim ricotta cheese
- 2 garlic cloves, minced
- Salt and freshly ground black pepper to taste

Directions:

1. Preheat the toaster oven to 375° F.
2. Layer the sheets of phyllo dough in an oiled or nonstick 9¾-inch-diameter baking pan, lightly brushing the top of each sheet with olive oil and folding in the corner edges to fit the pan.
3. Combine the topping mixture ingredients in a bowl and adjust the seasonings to taste. Spread the mixture on top of the phyllo pastry layers and sprinkle with the Parmesan cheese.
4. BAKE for 30 minutes, or until the cheese is melted and the topping is lightly browned. Remove carefully from the pan with a metal spatula.

Fresh Herb Veggie Pizza

Servings: 4

Cooking Time: 25 Minutes

Ingredients:

- 1 9-inch ready-made pizza crust
- 1 tablespoon olive oil
- 1 4-ounce can tomato paste
- 2 tablespoons shredded part-skim mozzarella
- 2 tablespoons grated Parmesan cheese
- 2 tablespoons crumbled feta cheese
- ½ bell pepper, chopped
- 1 tablespoon chopped fresh parsley
- 1 tablespoon chopped fresh oregano
- 1 tablespoon chopped fresh basil
- ½ teaspoon red pepper flakes
- Salt and freshly ground black pepper to taste
- Pizza mixture:
- 2 garlic cloves, minced
- 1 plum tomato, chopped

Directions:

1. Preheat the toaster oven to 400° F.
2. Brush the pizza crust with olive oil and spread the tomato paste evenly to cover.
3. Combine the ingredients for the pizza mixture and spread evenly on top of the tomato paste layer. Sprinkle the cheeses over all and season to taste. Place the pizza on the toaster oven rack.
4. BAKE for 25 minutes, or until the vegetables are cooked and the cheese is melted.

DESSERTS

Brownie Cookies

Servings: 3

Cooking Time: 9 Minutes

Ingredients:

- 2/3 cup shortening
- 1 1/2 cups brown sugar, packed
- 1 tablespoon water
- 1 teaspoon vanilla
- 2 eggs
- 1 1/3 cups flour
- 1/3 cup unsweetened baking cocoa
- 1/4 teaspoon baking soda
- 1/2 teaspoon salt
- 12 ounces semi-sweet chocolate chips

Directions:

1. Preheat the toaster oven to 375°F.
2. With flat beater, cream shortening and brown sugar on medium setting until blended.
3. Add water, vanilla, and eggs and mix. Add flour, cocoa, baking soda, and salt and beat at a medium setting until thoroughly mixed.
4. Stir in chocolate chips on low setting.
5. Drop tablespoons of dough on ungreased baking sheets.
6. Bake 7 to 9 minutes. Do not overcook.

Buttermilk Confetti Cake

Servings: 10-12

Cooking Time: 25 Minutes

Ingredients:

- 1 1/2 cups all purpose flour
- 1/2 teaspoon baking soda
- 1/4 teaspoon salt
- 1/2 cup butter, softened
- 1 cup sugar
- 1 teaspoon vanilla extract
- 2 large eggs
- 3/4 cup buttermilk
- 1/4 cup multi-colored sprinkle
- Cream Cheese Frosting
- Multi-colored sprinkles

Directions:

1. Preheat the toaster oven to 350°F. Grease two 8-inch cake pans and line with parchment paper.
2. Stir flour, baking soda and salt in small bowl. Set mixture aside.
3. Beat butter, sugar and vanilla extract on HIGH in large bowl until blended. Add eggs, one at a time, until well blended.
4. Alternately add flour mixture and buttermilk until combined. Stir in 1/4 cup sprinkles.
5. Divide batter evenly between prepared pans. Place one pan on bottom rack and one pan on top rack, rotate halfway through baking.
6. Bake 20 to 25 minutes or until a toothpick inserted in center of cakes comes out clean. Cool 10 minutes on wire rack.
7. Remove cakes from pans and cool completely on wire racks. Frost with Cream Cheese Frosting and top with sprinkles.

Campfire Banana Boats

Servings: 4

Cooking Time: 20 Minutes

Ingredients:

- 4 medium, unpeeled ripe bananas
- ¼ cup dark chocolate chips
- 4 teaspoons shredded, unsweetened coconut
- ½ cup mini marshmallows
- 4 graham crackers, chopped

Directions:

1. Preheat the toaster oven to 400°F on BAKE for 5 minutes.
2. Cut the bananas lengthwise through the skin about halfway through. Open the pocket to create a space for the other ingredients.
3. Evenly divide the chocolate, coconut, marshmallows, and graham crackers among the bananas.
4. Tear off four 12-inch squares of foil and place the bananas in the center of each. Crimp the foil around the banana to form a boat.
5. Place the bananas on the baking tray, two at a time, and in position 2, bake for 10 minutes until the fillings are gooey and the banana is warmed through.
6. Repeat with the remaining two bananas and serve.

Sour Cream Pound Cake

Servings: 6

Cooking Time: 60 Minutes

Ingredients:

- ¾ cup unsalted butter, plus extra for greasing the baking pan
- 2½ cups all-purpose flour, sifted, plus extra for dusting the baking pan
- 1½ cups granulated sugar
- 4 large eggs
- 2 teaspoons pure vanilla extract
- ½ teaspoon baking soda
- ¾ cup sour cream

Directions:

1. Place the rack in position 1 and preheat the toaster oven to 350°F on BAKE for 5 minutes.
2. Lightly grease and dust a 9-by-5-inch loaf pan.
3. In a large bowl, cream the butter and sugar with an electric hand beater until very light and fluffy, about 4 minutes.
4. Beat in the eggs one at a time, scraping down the sides of the bowl after each addition.
5. Beat in the vanilla.
6. In a medium bowl, stir the flour and baking soda.
7. Fold the flour mixture and sour cream into the butter mixture, alternating two times each, until well combined.
8. Spoon the batter into the loaf pan and bake for 1 hour, or until a toothpick inserted in the center comes out clean.
9. Let cool completely in the pan and serve.

Orange Strawberry Flan

Servings: 4

Cooking Time: 45 Minutes

Ingredients:

- ¼ cup sugar
- ½ cup concentrated orange juice
- 1 12-ounce can low-fat evaporated milk
- 3 egg yolks
- 1 cup frozen strawberries, thawed and sliced, or 1 cup fresh strawberries, washed, stemmed, and sliced
- 4 fresh mint sprigs

Directions:

1. Preheat the toaster oven to 375° F.
2. Place the sugar in a baking pan and broil for 4 minutes, or until the sugar melts. Remove from the oven, stir briefly, and pour equal portions of the caramelized sugar into four 1-cup-size ovenproof dishes. Set aside.
3. Blend the orange juice, evaporated milk, and egg yolks in a food processor or blender until smooth. Transfer the mixture to a medium bowl and fold in the sliced strawberries. Pour the mixture in equal portions into the four dishes.
4. BAKE for 45 minutes, or until a knife inserted in the center comes out clean. Chill for several hours. The flan may be loosened by running a knife around the edge and inverted on individual plates or served in the dishes. Garnish with fresh mint sprigs.

Frozen Brazo De Mercedes

Servings: 8

Cooking Time: 15 Minutes

Ingredients:

- 1 pint vanilla ice cream, softened to room temperature
- 1 (8 inch) premade graham cracker crust
- 6 large eggs, yolks and whites separated
- 7 ounces condensed milk
- ½ teaspoon vanilla extract
- ¼ teaspoon cream of tartar
- ⅓ cup granulated sugar

Directions:

1. Spread the ice cream on the bottom of the graham cracker crust in an even layer, cover with plastic wrap, and place in the freezer for 8 hours or overnight.
2. Whisk egg yolks and condensed milk over a double boiler continuously for 15 minutes or until the mixture becomes thick.
3. Whisk the vanilla extract into the egg mixture until fully combined.
4. Pass the custard through a fine sieve to remove any clumps.
5. Remove the ice cream and top with the egg yolk mixture, cover with plastic wrap, and place back into the freezer for 2 hours.
6. Beat the egg whites and cream of tartar in a stand mixer on high speed.
7. Add the sugar in slowly once the egg whites begin to foam.
8. Beat the egg whites for two minutes or until they form stiff peaks.
9. Remove the plastic wrap from the pie and top with the beaten egg whites.
10. Preheat the toaster Oven to 350°F.
11. Place the pie on the wire rack, then insert the rack at mid position in the preheated air fryer.
12. Select the Bake and Shake functions, adjust time to 15 minutes, and press Start/Pause.
13. Rotate the pie halfway through cooking for even browning. The Shake Reminder will let you know when.
14. Remove when done and place in the fridge for 1 hour, uncovered.
15. Cover the pie, then place in the freezer for 6 hours or overnight.
16. Remove the pie and allow it to rest at room temperature for 10 minutes, then slice and serve.

Blueberry Crumbles

Servings: 2

Cooking Time: 60 Minutes

Ingredients:

- 2 tablespoons granulated sugar
- 1½ teaspoons cornstarch
- ⅛ teaspoon table salt, divided
- 10 ounces (2 cups) blueberries
- ½ cup (1½ ounces) old-fashioned rolled oats
- ¼ cup (1¼ ounces) all-purpose flour
- ¼ cup packed (1¾ ounces) light brown sugar
- ¼ teaspoon ground cinnamon
- 4 tablespoons unsalted butter, melted and cooled

Directions:

1. Adjust toaster oven rack to lowest position and preheat the toaster oven to 375 degrees. Combine granulated sugar, cornstarch, and pinch salt in medium bowl. Gently toss blueberries in sugar mixture, then divide between two 12-ounce ramekins.
2. Combine oats, flour, brown sugar, cinnamon, and remaining pinch salt in now-empty bowl. Drizzle with melted butter and toss with fork until evenly moistened and mixture forms large chunks with some pea-size pieces throughout. Sprinkle topping evenly over blueberries, breaking up any large chunks.
3. Place ramekins on aluminum foil–lined small rimmed baking sheet and bake until filling is bubbling around edges and topping is deep golden brown, 25 to 30 minutes, rotating sheet halfway through baking. Let crumbles cool on wire rack for 15 minutes before serving.

Blueberry Crisp

Servings: 6

Cooking Time: 13 Minutes

Ingredients:

- 3 cups Fresh or thawed frozen blueberries
- ⅓ cup Granulated white sugar
- 1 tablespoon Instant tapioca
- ⅓ cup All-purpose flour
- ⅓ cup Rolled oats (not quick-cooking or steel-cut)
- ⅓ cup Chopped walnuts or pecans
- ⅓ cup Packed light brown sugar
- 5 tablespoons plus 1 teaspoon (⅔ stick) Butter, melted and cooled
- ¾ teaspoon Ground cinnamon
- ¼ teaspoon Table salt

Directions:

1. Preheat the toaster oven to 400°F.
2. Mix the blueberries, granulated white sugar, and instant tapioca in a 6-inch round cake pan for a small batch, a 7-inch round cake pan for a medium batch, or an 8-inch round cake pan for a large batch.
3. When the machine is at temperature, set the cake pan in the air fryer oven and air-fry undisturbed for 5 minutes, or just until the blueberries begin to bubble.
4. Meanwhile, mix the flour, oats, nuts, brown sugar, butter, cinnamon, and salt in a medium bowl until well combined.
5. When the blueberries have begun to bubble, crumble this flour mixture evenly on top. Continue air-frying undisturbed for 8 minutes, or until the topping has browned a bit and the filling is bubbling.
6. Use two hot pads or silicone baking mitts to transfer the cake pan to a wire rack. Cool for at least 10 minutes or to room temperature before serving.

Keto Cheesecake Cups

Servings: 6

Cooking Time: 10 Minutes

Ingredients:

- 8 ounces cream cheese
- ¼ cup plain whole-milk Greek yogurt
- 1 large egg
- 1 teaspoon pure vanilla extract
- 3 tablespoons monk fruit sweetener
- ¼ teaspoon salt
- ½ cup walnuts, roughly chopped

Directions:

1. Preheat the toaster oven to 315°F.
2. In a large bowl, use a hand mixer to beat the cream cheese together with the yogurt, egg, vanilla, sweetener, and salt. When combined, fold in the chopped walnuts.
3. Set 6 silicone muffin liners inside an air-fryer-safe pan.
4. Evenly fill the cupcake liners with cheesecake batter.
5. Carefully place the pan into the air fryer oven and air-fry for about 10 minutes, or until the tops are lightly browned and firm.
6. Carefully remove the pan when done and place in the refrigerator for 3 hours to firm up before serving.

Apple Juice Piecrust

Servings: 4

Cooking Time: 10 Minutes

Ingredients:

- 1¼ cups unbleached flour
- ¼ cup margarine
- ¼ cup apple juice
- Pinch of grated nutmeg
- Salt to taste

Directions:

1. Preheat the toaster oven to 350° F.
2. Cut together the flour and margarine with a knife or pastry cutter until the mixture is crumbly. Add the apple juice, nutmeg, and salt and cut again to blend. Turn the dough out onto a lightly floured surface and knead for 2 minutes. Roll out into a circle large enough to fit a 9¾-inch pie pan. Pierce in several places to prevent bubbling and press the tines of a fork around the rim to decorate the crust edge.
3. BAKE for 10 minutes, or until lightly browned.

www.ingramcontent.com/pod-product-compliance
Ingram Content Group UK Ltd.
Pitfield, Milton Keynes, MK11 3LW, UK
UKHW051133260726
13967UKWH00010B/3013

9 781803 202839